Bullying Issues

ISSUES

Volume 165

Series Editor

Lisa Firth

Independence

Educational Publishers
Cambridge

First published by Independence
The Studio, High Green
Great Shelford
Cambridge CB22 5EG
England

© Independence 2009

British Library Cataloguing in Publication Data
Bullying Issues – (Issues Series)
I. Bullying II. Bullying in the workplace III. Firth, Lisa
302.3

ISBN 978 1 86168 469 1

Printed in Great Britain
MWL Print Group Ltd

Cover
The illustration on the front cover is by
Don Hatcher.

CONTENTS

Chapter One: Bullying Trends

Chapter Two: Cyberbullying

Chapter Three: Bullying at Work

Useful information for readers

Dear Reader,

Issues: Bullying Issues

It is estimated that 31% of children will suffer some form of bullying during childhood. Adults are also not immune, with workplace bullying costing employers an estimated £3bn a year. The rise of communications technology means victims are finding that even at home they are not safe from their attackers, with cyberbullies increasingly targeting them via the Internet and mobile phones. This book gives a comprehensive overview of this traumatic issue.

The purpose of *Issues*

Bullying Issues is the one hundred and sixty-fifth volume in the **Issues** series. The aim of this series is to offer up-to-date information about important issues in our world. Whether you are a regular reader or new to the series, we do hope you find this book a useful overview of the many and complex issues involved in the topic. This title replaces an older volume in the **Issues** series, Volume 122: **Bullying,** which is now out of print.

Titles in the **Issues** series are resource books designed to be of especial use to those undertaking project work or requiring an overview of facts, opinions and information on a particular subject, particularly as a prelude to undertaking their own research.

The information in this book is not from a single author, publication or organisation; the value of this unique series lies in the fact that it presents information from a wide variety of sources, including:

⇨ Government reports and statistics
⇨ Newspaper articles and features
⇨ Information from think-tanks and policy institutes
⇨ Magazine features and surveys
⇨ Website material
⇨ Literature from lobby groups and charitable organisations.*

Critical evaluation

Because the information reprinted here is from a number of different sources, readers should bear in mind the origin of the text and whether the source is likely to have a particular bias or agenda when presenting information (just as they would if undertaking their own research). It is hoped that, as you read about the many aspects of the issues explored in this book, you will critically evaluate the information presented. It is important that you decide whether you are being presented with facts or opinions. Does the writer give a biased or an unbiased report? If an opinion is being expressed, do you agree with the writer?

Bullying Issues offers a useful starting point for those who need convenient access to information about the many issues involved. However, it is only a starting point. Following each article is a URL to the relevant organisation's website, which you may wish to visit for further information.

Kind regards,

Lisa Firth
Editor, **Issues** series

** Please note that Independence Publishers has no political affiliations or opinions on the topics covered in the **Issues** series, and any views quoted in this book are not necessarily those of the publisher or its staff.*

Bullying

Information from the NSPCC

Definition

Bullying is the persistent, intentional harming of another person with an unequal power relationship. The types of bullying fall into a number of categories, including verbal, physical, emotional and non-verbal.

Bullying is not confined to school; bullying happens in the home and other areas of a child's life, particularly in places where children congregate. Increasingly, bullying is happening via text message and online.

Key dates

⇨ Since December 1999 all schools must have an anti-bullying policy in place by law.

31% of children experienced bullying during childhood, a further 7% were discriminated against and 14% were made to feel an outsider

⇨ Since April 2004 all schools and LEAs have a duty to make arrangements to safeguard and promote the welfare of children.

Key points

⇨ Children who are bullied can suffer immense emotional and physical trauma, sometimes with lasting effects.
⇨ Children can be bullied for a number of reasons including appearance, race, religion, social background, disability or sexuality.
⇨ People bully for a variety of reasons. They may have been bullied themselves, have low self-esteem or confidence.

⇨ The NSPCC believes that the most effective anti-bullying strategies in school are those that involve all members of the school community.
⇨ Strategies should be preventive as well as reactive and be supportive of the victim. However, it is also important to work with the bully because intervention works better than punishment.
⇨ It is important for young people to participate in anti-bullying strategies. In addition those working with children should communicate to children and young people the impact bullying can have and why they should actively intervene to prevent it.
⇨ The NSPCC chairs the Anti-Bullying Alliance. The Alliance brings together 50 organisations from the voluntary, educational, professional and private sectors to tackle the problem of bullying and create safer environments for children and young people.

Statistics

⇨ 31% of children experienced bullying during childhood, a further 7% were discriminated against and 14% were made to feel different/an outsider. 43% experienced at least one of these things during childhood. (Cawson et al., 2000, *Child Maltreatment in the UK: A Study of the Prevalence of Child Abuse and Neglect*, NSPCC, p.26)
⇨ A quarter of young adults bullied by their peers during childhood report that they suffered long term harmful effects as a result. (Cawson et al., 2000, *Child Maltreatment in the UK: A Study of the Prevalence of Child Abuse and Neglect*, NSPCC, p.30)
⇨ 54% of both primary and secondary school children thought that bullying was 'a big problem' or 'quite a big problem' in their school. (Oliver and Kandappa, 2003, *Tackling Bullying: Listening to the views of children and young people – Summary Report*, Thomas Coram Research Unit, Institute of Education)
⇨ Around a third of boys (35%) and a quarter of girls (26%) admit they have bullied other children 'a little' and/or 'a lot'. (Katz et al., 2001, *Bullying in Britain: Testimonies from Teenagers*, Young Voice, p.9)

⇨ 30% of children did not tell anyone that they had been bullied. (Smith and Shu, 2000, 'What Good Schools Can Do About Bullying: Findings from a survey in English Schools after a decade of research and action', *Childhood*, 7:2, pp.193-212, p.204)

⇨ Research with 11- to 19-year-olds found that 1 in 5 young people (20%) had experienced bullying or threats via email, Internet chatroom or text message. Bullying using text messaging was the most common of these three forms of bullying, experienced by 14% of young people. Almost three-quarters (73%) of young people who had been bullied by email, Internet chatroom or text message said they knew the person who bullied or threatened them, while a quarter (26%) said it was done by a stranger.

⇨ A study of more than 11,000 secondary school pupils from 2002 to 2005 asked them how often they had received any nasty or threatening text messages or emails showed an increase year on year. (Noret, N and Rivers, I, 2006. *The prevalence of bullying by text message or email: Results of a four-year study* poster presented at British Psychological Society Annual Conference, Cardiff, April

⇨ A recent survey which asked 1,145 young people who are lesbian, gay or bisexual (or think they might be) about their experiences of school found that:

↳ Almost two-thirds (65 per cent) of young lesbian, gay and bisexual pupils have experienced direct bullying.

↳ Seventy-five per cent of young gay people attending faith schools have experienced bullying.

↳ Over half of lesbian and gay pupils don't feel able to be themselves at school. Thirty-five per cent of gay pupils do not feel safe or accepted at school.

↳ Less than a quarter (23 per cent) of young gay people have been told that homophobic bullying is wrong in their school. In schools that have said homophobic bullying is wrong, gay young people are 60 per cent more likely not to have been bullied. (Hunt, R and Johan Jensen, 2007, *The School Report: The experiences of young gay people in Britain's schools*, Stonewall.)

⇨ Children and young people with a learning disability are twice as likely to be bullied as able-bodied children. Recent research by Mencap (2007) found that 82% of children and young people with a learning disability have experienced bullying. (Mencap, 2007, *Bullying wrecks lives: the experiences of children and young people with a learning disability*) September 2008

⇨ The above information is a journalistic briefing from the NSPCC and is reprinted with permission. Visit www.nspcc.org.uk for more information.

© NSPCC

Expert guide: bullying

Information from Community Care

A floral tribute from 16-year-old Karl Peart's teacher at his funeral in June read: 'I hope you find the peace you longed for. I tried to keep you safe, but my efforts were in vain.'

Karl is one of three children to commit suicide in the last few weeks because they were being bullied at school. He is believed to have taken a mixture of painkillers and alcohol after being bullied through primary school and regularly attacked at secondary school.

The same month, Christopher O'Reilly, aged 15, was found hanged by his Leeds United scarf in his bedroom by his mother. And a couple of weeks later, 11-year-old Thomas Thompson took an overdose of painkillers after being bullied for a number of years at school for being 'too clever', his family said. He died before reaching hospital.

Meanwhile, the parents of nine-year-old Jessica O'Connell removed her from school after being told that a fellow pupil who had bullied their daughter would only be suspended for a day because the bullying was 'not serious enough'.

In all schools, at least 5-10 per cent of pupils will experience long-term, persistent bullying, but in some schools this figure will be higher

----

Jessica chronicled the bullying in her diary. One entry reads that a pupil 'threatened to kill me if I didn't let her hit me so I had to let her hit me because I didn't want to die'. Another entry says: 'I wish I was dead so I don't have to suffer any more pain.'

And just this week, Sarah Fisher revealed that she had lost her voice for almost a year because she was so traumatised by being bullied at school. The 16-year-old can still only speak in a whisper, and then only for short periods of time. Sarah had been repeatedly called names and pushed and shoved at school. The bullying worsened after she lost her voice. She is now looking forward to starting at a new college.

Schools have a legal duty to prevent all forms of bullying and to have anti-bullying strategies in place. Earlier this year, ministers announced a £470 million behaviour and attendance programme in a bid to crack down on school bullying. Proposals include funding and training for all secondary schools in anti-bullying strategies and specialist consultants to help

local education authorities tackle the problem.

However, in all schools, at least 5-10 per cent of pupils will experience long-term, persistent bullying, but in some schools this figure will be higher. Bullying can take several forms, including:

⇨ name-calling and teasing;
⇨ being pushed, hit or attacked;
⇨ having your bag or other possessions taken and thrown about or stolen;
⇨ having rumours spread about you;
⇨ being ignored and left out;
⇨ being forced to hand over money.

There are several factors that make bullying more likely:

⇨ lacking close friends in school;
⇨ being shy;
⇨ an over protective family environment;

⇨ being from a different racial or ethnic group to the majority;
⇨ being different in some respect, for example, stammering;
⇨ having special educational needs or a disability;
⇨ having expensive accessories such as mobile phone or computer games.

For six years, bullying has been the biggest single reason for children calling ChildLine, with about 20,000 calls a year. The recent report 'Tackling Bullying' sponsored by ChildLine, funded by the department for education and skills and conducted by the Thomas Coram Research Unit, found that over half of primary and secondary school pupils thought bullying was a big problem in their school.

Just over half of pupils in Year 5 said they had been bullied during the term, compared with 28 per cent of pupils in Year 8. Over 60 per cent of pupils thought their school was good at dealing with bullying.

Name-calling was the most prevalent form of bullying. A minority of pupils reported sexist, racist and homophobic abuse. Nasty messages sent by text on mobile phones or through emails is emerging as the latest form of bullying.

In 1999, the then DfEE said: 'The emotional distress caused by bullying in whatever form – be it racial, or as a result of a child's appearance, behaviour or special educational needs, or related to sexual orientation – can prejudice school achievement, lead to lateness or truancy, and in extreme cases, end with suicide...Low report rates should not themselves be taken as proof that bullying is not occurring.' *25 April 2008*

⇨ The above information is reprinted with kind permission from Community Care. Visit www.communitycare.co.uk for more.

© Community Care

Children on bullying

An extract from a report by the Children's Rights Director for England

What is bullying?

Findings

⇨ Whether something is bullying depends on how it affects the person, not on what is being done.

In many of our discussion groups we heard that being forced to do something you don't want to do can be bullying

---

⇨ Something is bullying if it hurts someone who can't defend themselves and doesn't deserve what happens to them.
⇨ Something unpleasant that is done

to a child by a group of others, or that is repeated, is more likely to count as bullying.

⇨ Bullying is a mixture of physical violence and verbal hurting.
⇨ Children, like people in any group, will pull themselves up in the group by pushing others down. That is not bullying unless someone is just putting one person down instead of pushing for their own position in the group.
⇨ Joking, teasing, arguing, play fighting and name calling are not always bullying – but they can be if they affect someone badly.
⇨ Adults sometimes get it wrong when they decide what is bullying and what is not bullying, because they don't take into account how it affects the child.
⇨ The law is more likely to punish

adults who bully other adults than children who bully other children.

People have different ideas about what counts as being bullied, so we asked children what they thought. This question was answered by 150 children. Here are their top answers.

What is bullying?

⇨ Being physically violent to someone (hitting them or beating them up) (59%).
⇨ Calling someone names (45%).
⇨ Making teasing or hurtful comments that put someone down (25%).
⇨ Ganging up to pick on someone (12%).
⇨ Threatening someone (7%).

Nine children wrote on their cards that discrimination counted as bullying. Eight wrote that anything that actually makes someone else feel sad or uncomfortable counts as bullying. Four wrote that taking people's property by force was a type of bullying.

In many of our discussion groups we heard that being forced to do something you don't want to do can be bullying. One group told us that one example of this is peer pressure to take drugs. Other groups said bullying includes blackmail and sexual abuse. One discussion group defined bullying as 'purposeful intimidation of a person'. Another defined it as 'deliberately or not deliberately making someone feel bad about themselves', or 'an unnecessary act to hurt someone'.

We heard that actions that may seem small to some people can be bullying for others. This could include 'people making fun of you'. Many spoke strongly about being excluded from the group as being a definite form of bullying. We heard that being ignored can make someone feel worthless.

Children told us three main things that can make anything count as bullying. One thing is not so much what is actually done, but the bad effect on the person being bullied: 'anything that has a serious impact on someone'; 'anything which hurts or makes anyone feel bad'. The second is that the person being bullied cannot easily defend themselves against the bully or bullies: 'picking on someone that can't defend themselves'; 'picking on someone younger or with a disability'. The third is that the person being bullied does not

deserve how they are being treated: 'picking on a person who has done nothing'; 'picks on someone for no reason or for attention'.

It can also make a difference if what is being said or done is by a group rather than by just one person. Children told us that it is more likely to be bullying if there is a group involved. We also heard that something that happens just once might not have a big effect or be bullying, but the same thing being repeated lots of times can be real bullying.

In one of our discussion groups, young people described how people will struggle to join a group and then struggle for a good position in that group. They said this has to be accepted because it happens in all groups of people. If someone is only pushing to improve their own position, 'it's not bullying because it's not personal'. They said it is natural for each person in a group to try to pull themselves up by pushing others down, and to make friends in a group by putting weaker people down. They saw this as the natural survival of the fittest in any group of people, but it can become bullying if someone is trying to do one particular person down instead of just struggling for their own position amongst everyone else. The discussion group said it is not easy to tell where the line is between competition for friends, resources or space and real bullying.

We asked whether there are some things that people often call bullying, but that the children thought didn't count. Out of the 95 people who wrote about this, 21 (over one in five) told us that everything that is often called bullying really does count as bullying for them. 'If someone feels they are bullied, they usually are.'

Over a quarter (27 children) told us they thought that 'joking around' often gets counted wrongly as bullying, but some said it depended on how people felt about the joking. Sometimes a joke 'goes beyond what was intended'. People just saying 'joke' if they think they have gone too far doesn't change the fact that they might have just bullied someone.

In our discussion groups, children told us that something said in a teasing way by a friend may have no effect at all, but the same thing said by someone else can offend or upset you. Sometimes though, teasing by a friend can turn into something bigger and a child can lose friends and become a victim if they react badly to teasing.

Fifteen of the children who answered this question on our cards told us that simply arguing with someone sometimes wrongly gets counted as bullying. This included friends arguing or falling out with one another. Eight children wrote that not talking to someone, which can happen when friends fall out with each other, also sometimes gets wrongly called bullying. Nine children wrote that play-fighting sometimes gets wrongly called bullying. Many in our discussion groups told us that real fighting is often a type of bullying, though.

Although 67 children wrote that name calling is definitely bullying, 7 children disagreed with this, and wrote that name calling is one of the things that sometimes gets wrongly called bullying. One wrote that 'calling people names is not bullying because you can just ignore it', but another wrote that it depends how the person being called names feels about it. In discussion, we heard that teasing is supposed to be funny, but in order to be funny it can have a very cruel edge to it.

We heard in our discussions that adults in charge of children will often say 'this is bullying' or 'this isn't bullying'. Children told us that this is not right, because the adults who say that do not take into account how different people are sensitive to different things. Whether something is bullying depends a lot on how it affects the person not just on what is being said or done.

One discussion group thought that things that happen often in everyday life should not be counted as bullying. An example was pushing in front of someone in a queue. Another was doing something because of peer pressure. We heard that peer pressure is why many people do lots of things, and doesn't count as bullying unless it involves intimidation.

Issues

www.independence.co.uk

One group reminded us that some sorts of bullying of children are against the law. A second group said that the law might punish adults who seriously bully other adults, but not children and young people who bully other children and young people. A third group agreed with the person who said 'if you do a crime you go to prison or a detention centre but for bullying there's nothing, but it's probably higher coz it affects people's lives'.

Over a quarter (27 children) told us they thought that 'joking around' often gets counted wrongly as bullying

---

What happened last time the children were bullied?

We asked children and young people who had been bullied recently to tell us exactly what had happened to them the last time they got bullied. Sixty-five children answered this question on the cards. Here are the three most usual types of bullying that had happened to those children:

The most common ways of being bullied

⇨ Name calling (42%).
⇨ Being hit (25%).
⇨ Being beaten up (15%).

Children and young people can experience different forms of bullying at different times. It is clear that the children who answered this question had experienced both verbal bullying (mainly being called names) and physical violence of one sort or another. Children living in children's homes were more likely to have been physically bullied than those in foster care. For six children, their last experience of bullying was being threatened, for five it was being 'put down' by others, and for five it was being teased.

For three children, their last experience of bullying had been racism, and for two the last time they had been bullied it was cyberbullying. Although we cannot be sure from the figures, it looks as if cyberbullying is often mixed in with other sorts of bullying: 19 children had told us on their question cards that they had at some time been bullied in this way, but only two said that it was the last sort of bullying to have happened to them.

What triggers bullying?

Findings

⇨ Bullying can be triggered by arguing with a bully or something small angering a bully.
⇨ If you are seen as different from other children, bullies may bully you whenever they feel like it.
⇨ Bullying can grow from banter, jealousy, or trying to get someone to react to being wound up.
⇨ Bullying can be a revenge for reporting earlier bullying.

On the question cards, 118 children told us what sorts of things usually trigger a bullying incident. Here are their most usual answers:

What usually sets bullying off?

⇨ Someone arguing with a bully (41%).
⇨ Something, however small, that angers a bully (32%).
⇨ Just being different from other children (27%).

In our discussions we heard that you can anger a bully by something as small as accidentally tripping them up in a game or looking at them in the wrong way. We also heard that if you are seen as different in some way from the other children, bullying can happen to you without anything in particular setting it off. Someone who is seen as different risks getting bullied whenever bullies feel like it. We also heard that a bully can attack you to get their own back if they find out you have told someone about them: 'if they think you're a tell tale they might start doing it to you'.

Discussion groups talked a lot about how bullying can start and grow. One group described how bullying can start with banter within a group, then this can go too far and someone feels hurt by it. When they show they are affected, they are seen as someone who 'can't take banter', and laughed at. They are then verbally teased about this, which turns into verbal bullying, which keeps going if they react and get upset by it.

Another group described bullying that begins with someone being jealous of someone else's successes, abilities or possessions, and begins to hurt them as a result. When someone feels down and finds that the only way of pulling themselves up is by putting someone else down, bullying will grow and get worse.

Yet another group described how bullying can start with people trying, as a sort of challenge, to wind someone up until they react in an extreme way. If that works, the same people will try again and again to get that person to react even more extremely, and probably before long will get them into trouble for how they react, perhaps in front of staff.

To get more detail, we asked what had triggered the bullying the last time it had happened. We did not suggest any reasons. Seventy-two children answered this question. The most common reasons we were given included the child being an easy target (nine children), looking or being different from the other children in some way (nine children), the bullies simply not liking the person they bullied (seven children), and the bullies already being angry for some reason (seven children).

Six children wrote that the bullies had simply bullied them for fun the last time they had been bullied, and another six thought the bullies were jealous of them for one reason or another. One person told us that the last time they had been bullied it was because they had been trying to help someone else who was being bullied, and the bullies had turned on them.

Nineteen of the children (just over a quarter) who told us about the last time they were bullied said they just didn't know why they had been bullied that time. One person wrote that they had been bullied the last time for 'me being alive'.

14 February 2008

⇨ The above information is taken from *Children on bullying – a report by the Children's Rights Director for England* and is reprinted with kind permission from Ofsted. Visit www.ofsted.gov.uk for more information.

© Crown copyright

Bullying myths and facts

Information from respectme

There are a lot of different ideas about bullying flying around. This article is to help you to separate the myths that there are about bullying and provide you with the facts. One of the main facts to remember is that every child has the right not to be bullied – that includes you.

Myth – Bullying is a normal part of growing up

Bullying is not a normal part of growing up and it's not part of any character-building process. Adults do not expect to be hit, tripped and poked or called names and threatened when they go to work. You have this same right to be free from bullying and to feel safe wherever you are.

Bullying can make you feel depressed or lonely, it can affect your school work and make you dread going to school – this is not normal, you shouldn't have to feel like this.

Myth – People bring bullying on themselves because of their behaviour

No one deserves to be bullied and no one makes someone bully them. You have the right to be yourself, to wear what you want, to form your own opinions and be who you want to be without fear of being targeted by bullies.

Life would be dull if everyone was the same. Differences make life interesting and they should be respected.

Myth – Only weak people are bullied

Bullying is about perception – how someone is viewed by other people. People may be seen as being weak because they do not play a particular sport, they are shy, or they are the new person at a school. This does not mean that a person is weak, bullies tend to pick on people that they feel they may have power over.

Myth – Bullying only takes place at school – teachers should deal with it

Bullying can take place anywhere, both inside and outside of the school gates. This can include football practice, Girl Guides, Scouts, local youth club, parks and local transport. Yes, teachers should and can deal with it but so should all other adults – your parents, youth leaders, bus drivers, local police and even you – everyone has a role to play in tackling bullying.

Myth – There's nothing I can do to stop someone else being bullied

You can play an important role in stopping bullying. Refuse to join in with any bullying behaviour – but remember that by doing nothing people might think that you agree with the bullying. So, keep safe but do something. Tell a trusted adult about the behaviour. Get involved with any anti-bullying schemes you know of, such as buddy schemes, peer counselling or helping raise awareness of bullying through poster campaigns and school assemblies.

Myth – Bullying is only physical in nature

Physical acts such as hitting, kicking and pushing is bullying but bullying can also take many different forms. This can include:

⇨ Being ignored, left out or having rumours spread about you.

⇨ Having belongings stolen or damaged.

⇨ Being called names, teased, put down or threatened.

⇨ Receiving abusive text messages or emails.

⇨ Being targeted for who you are or who you are perceived to be.

Although bullying behaviour can be different, each 'type' of bullying is just as hurtful and upsetting as the next. You have the right not to be bullied.

Myth – Telling will only make it worse – it's grassing and adults will just overreact

There is a difference between telling on someone to get them into trouble and telling on someone to help other people. If you or someone else you know is being bullied, the best way to make it stop is to let an adult know what is happening. Pick an adult that you know and trust and if you are worried about them overreacting explain your fears to them and why. The last thing that any adult will want to do is make the situation and bullying worse, so be open and honest about what you would like to happen.

⇨ The above information is reprinted with kind permission from respectme. Visit www.respectme.org.uk for more information.

© respectme

Survey finds one in three bullied outside school

Information from the National Children's Bureau

The Anti-Bullying Alliance releases the results of its annual poll of children and young people today to mark the start of Anti-Bullying Week 2007.

The 2007 Anti-Bullying Week campaign focuses on 'bullying in the community' with the message 'safer together, safer wherever', to remind us that we all have a role to play in keeping children and young people safe wherever they are.

This year's poll shows that 35% of a sample of 7- to 18-year-olds say that they have been bullied outside of school. The survey carried out by BMRB for the ABA with 1,078 7- to 18-year-olds in England, found that the most likely places for children and young people to experience bullying outside school were on the street (16%), on the way to and from school, and in the park (12%).

The majority also (55%) thought that about half or more of the bullying that happens in school actually starts outside of school and 4 in 10 said bullying outside of school was more worrying as adults weren't around to help. However, more than half reported that they would tell an adult in school if they were bullied outside of school.

Chris Cloke, ABA Chair, said: 'We must think carefully about what children and young people are telling us. Clearly, whilst we welcome the finding that a significant majority felt safe when they were out in their communities, more than a third had experienced bullying – this is simply unacceptable. Young people also draw a critical link here between bullying in school and bullying that starts out in the community or which may be exacerbated by community conflicts or local feuds. We need to support our schools in responding to this challenge, which is a significant one.'

The poll also found that:

⇨ Young people over the age of 15 reported more bullying than younger children, with 1 in 5 experiencing bullying on the streets of their community.

⇨ Just over half young people said they would talk about bullying outside of school to friends and parents/carers, and 30% said another family member. 1 in 10 stated they would talk to the police.

⇨ Worryingly, 6% said they would keep it to themselves and not turn to anyone for help.

In this year's Anti-Bullying Week pack for schools, ABA highlighted research* identified four main types of behaviour that constitute bullying outside of the school space as: barging in, extortion, intimidation and name calling.

Mark Vickers, Headteacher of Manhood Community College in West Sussex, said: 'Bullying in the community is an issue for us all, not just for schools. There is a growing need for outside agencies, community partners, parents and carers and school leaders to work together to ensure that our communities are kind and cohesive and that children are safe, secure and supported. That is a responsibility we all share.'

To date bullying outside of school has been under-researched,** so this survey is very important in helping us find out more about what children and young people really think about the issue. This survey has shown us that bullying outside of school is a significant problem. Whilst some children and young people feel able to turn to an adult for help, many still do not, and we need to change that.

With Anti-Bullying Week 2007 ABA aims to raise awareness of the damage bullying can cause, and to give teachers, parents, children and young people the message that together we can stop it.

Typical answers given to the question 'What would have helped you deal with being bullied in the community?'

Support in the community

⇨ 'Having more community groups around'

⇨ 'People keeping an eye out on younger children and helping if they could'

⇨ 'If more support was given from people in the community'

⇨ 'More patrolling police officers'

⇨ 'A community centre in the local area'

Support from adults
⇨ 'An adult to tell straight away'
⇨ 'Support to get through it'
⇨ 'Being able to talk to someone in confidence'
⇨ 'To see an adult ask if anything is going on or to see if there is a problem or if everything is ok?'
⇨ 'They stopped when I say I would tell an adult'

Support from school
⇨ 'Teachers paying a bit more attention to it'
⇨ 'My teacher helps me if I am in trouble, and also a dinner lady'
⇨ 'I think that schools should help more with bullying outside of school'

⇨ 'Make sure it gets sorted out straight away by school'
⇨ 'Have a safe area for children who are being bullied'

Support getting to and from school safely
⇨ 'Someone to oversee on the bus'
⇨ 'Someone on the bus'
⇨ 'A bus conductor'
⇨ 'Not walking alone'
⇨ 'Getting a teacher to come on the bus with you'

Notes
* Percy-Smith, B & Matthews, H. (2001) 'Tyrannical spaces: Young people, bullying and urban neighbourhoods', *Local Environment*, 6, 49-63
** Taken from a review carried out

by the Research & Evaluation Team of ABA, based at the Unit for School and Family Studies, Goldsmiths College, University of London.
⇨ The Anti-Bullying Week survey was carried out for the Anti-Bullying Alliance by BMRB during September-October 2007 with 1,078 7- to 18-year-olds in England.
15 November 2007

⇨ The above information is re-printed with kind permission from the National Children's Bureau. Visit www.anti-bullyingalliance.org.uk for more information on this and other related topics.

© National Children's Bureau

Prejudice-related bullying

Information from NASUWT

Defining the problem

Prejudice-related bullying is a social problem which has its roots within wider social discourses that seek to justify negative behaviours against particular groups within society. Prejudice-related bullying is often characterised by abusive behaviour, intolerance or ostracism on grounds of an individual's gender, ethnicity, body image/size, sexuality, disability, age, religion or belief. Prejudice-related bullying implies not only that individuals may be targeted by bullies on grounds of their identity and social characteristics; it may also be the case that individual bullies form alliances with other individuals who they believe to have common interests and a common identity. Given its roots, effective strategies to tackle prejudice-related bullying require concerted action across all spheres of society, as well as in schools and colleges, to create a climate in which difference and diversity are recognised, respected and celebrated.

Bullying that is prejudice-related can include verbal and physical assaults, threats, offensive 'jokes' or language, mockery and ridicule, insulting or abusive behaviour and gestures, graffiti, and theft and

damage to property. It can also include the exclusion of others on grounds of their identity or characteristics. In particular, it should be noted that prejudice-related bullying is based on irrational views, beliefs and fears, leading to dislike and hatred of different individuals and groups.

Schools and colleges need to have in place effective systems to deal specifically with the problem of prejudice-related bullying. School and college anti-bullying policies and procedures should include specific reference to prejudice-related bullying in all its forms, including bullying on grounds of body image/size/

obesity; homophobic bullying; racist bullying; faith-based bullying; ageist bullying; disability bullying; and sexist bullying.

Bullying on grounds of body image/size/obesity

Bullying on the grounds of body image/size/obesity is one of the most prevalent forms of prejudice-related bullying. Recently, the level of such bullying has been exacerbated by national concerns about rising levels of obesity. Research suggests that children who are perceived to be overweight are often considered to be inferior and less valued than others

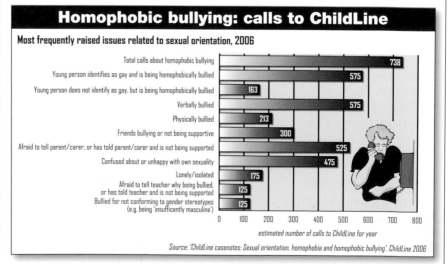

Homophobic bullying: calls to ChildLine

Most frequently raised issues related to sexual orientation, 2006

Issue	estimated number of calls to ChildLine for year
Total calls about homophobic bullying	738
Young person identifies as gay and is being homophobically bullied	575
Young person does not identify as gay, but is being homophobically bullied	163
Verbally bullied	575
Physically bullied	213
Friends bullying or not being supportive	300
Afraid to tell parent/carer, or has told parent/carer and is not being supported	525
Confused about or unhappy with own sexuality	475
Lonely/isolated	175
Afraid to tell teacher why being bullied, or has told teacher and is not being supported	125
Bullied for not conforming to gender stereotypes (e.g. being 'insufficiently masculine')	125

Source: 'ChildLine casenotes: Sexual orientation, homophobia and homophobic bullying'. ChildLine 2006

in educational and social terms. The media's constant reinforcement of concerns about body image/size/obesity and the trivialisation of these issues is a key factor related to this problem.

Homophobic bullying

Homophobic bullying is increasingly recognised as a widespread problem in schools and colleges and is the second most prevalent reason for bullying of pupils/students. Given the nature of this bullying, however, many individuals who are bullied may be unwilling to report the problem to parents, staff or colleagues since they may fear being further stigmatised and isolated. The problem of homophobia is often a hidden problem, because individuals may be unwilling to talk about it and may not feel safe in doing so. Research indicates that more than half of lesbian and gay young people had been subjected to homophobic bullying during their time at school or college.

Racist bullying

Bullying and harassment on racist grounds is a persistent issue that affects schools and colleges, including those where there are relatively few pupils or staff from black and minority ethnic groups. It is distinct from bullying on grounds of religion/belief. Racist bullying is often directed against individuals based on skin colour but might also include bullying against individuals because of their ethnic or national origin. The Race Relations (Amendment) Act 2000 requires local authorities, schools and colleges to establish a specific policy on promoting racial equality, to monitor the impact of this policy and to monitor and record racist bullying. Schools and colleges in areas where there is organised racist or fascist activity may also need additional support from local authorities, trade unions and other bodies to ensure that pupils/students and staff are protected.

Faith-based bullying

Faith-based bullying is directed against individuals and groups because of their religious belief or affiliation. It may also include bullying behaviour directed against individuals who are of no faith. The problem of faith-based bullying in schools and colleges has intensified in recent years, particularly in the case of anti-Muslim prejudice and racism. Prejudice-related bullying on grounds of religion or belief is also exacerbated by sectarian divisions in schools/colleges and society.

Ageist bullying

Ageist bullying is directed against individuals on the grounds of their age, and may be targeted at younger or older pupils/students and staff, often leading to exclusion from the social group or network.

Prejudice-related bullying is a social problem which has its roots within wider social discourses that seek to justify negative behaviours against particular groups within society

---

Disability bullying

Bullying on grounds of disability, like other forms of prejudice-related bullying, is linked to irrational and unfounded beliefs, assumptions and stereotypes about the disabled person and her/his abilities.

Sexist bullying

Sexist bullying is most commonly directed against girls and women. It is influenced by a range of factors, including in the media and the home. Research indicates that the emotional wellbeing of children and young people who experience domestic violence in the home is seriously affected, and this has a deleterious effect on their capacity to learn and on their behaviour.

Cyberbullying – a new tool of the bully

The development of information communications technology (ICT) has seen a rapid increase in new forms of bullying behaviours. With wider access to, and availability of, the Internet, email and mobile telephones, cyberbullying and associated threatening behaviour (cyber threats) are emerging as key challenges for schools and colleges. Between a fifth and a quarter of students have been cyber bullied at least once and the problem is more likely to occur outside rather than inside schools/colleges. A significant minority of those who are bullied tell no one about the bullying.

Cyberbullying may include threats and intimidation directed against staff as well as pupils and jeopardises effective teaching and learning. All schools and colleges should have in place disciplinary policies and procedures which address the problem of cyberbullying to protect pupils/students and staff, and to regulate the use of ICT equipment inside and outside the school or college.

⇨ The above information is re-printed with kind permission from NASUWT. Visit www.nasuwt.org.uk for more information.

© NASUWT

'I was called names like slut and whore'

Sexual bullying can ruin children's lives, but little is done to tackle it. Emine Saner looks at one campaign that aims to change attitudes among both sexes

A 16-year-old girl in Cornwall was repeatedly called a 'slapper' because she had a large bust; she eventually had a breast reduction in the hope that the bullying would stop. A 14-year-old girl in Essex endured months of being called a 'slag' and a 'skank' and contemplated suicide; one day about 30 teenagers set on her, pulling her top down and exposing her breasts. She was beaten up so badly she was in hospital for three days. A 16-year-old schoolboy was charged with sexually assaulting a 14-year-old girl, and another was charged for filming the attack and distributing the pictures on his mobile phone. These are just a few of the cases of sexual bullying that have been reported during the past few years.

Sexual bullying can be used to describe anything from sexualised comments about appearance and name-calling, such as 'slag', to spreading rumours about someone's sexual behaviour, to criminal offences such as assault and rape. 'Things are happening in schools that would never be allowed to happen in the workplace,' says Maria Banos Smith from the charity Womankind

Worldwide. 'Yet schools are public institutions and kids don't have any choice about whether they are there or not.'

Like any kind of bullying, it can ruin the lives of the victims, but the sexual dimension of gender bullying means it can be even harder to talk about and so is rarely addressed. Sarah, 17, was bullied by a group of boys as soon as she started secondary school. 'I was called names like "slut" and "whore" – those were terms most boys used against girls,' she says. 'I was shy and I wore clothes that covered me up, and a group of boys would always ask me to take off my jumper, open up my shirt a bit, or tell me I should be wearing skirts so they could see my legs. A group of boys would grab me in corridors – it was embarrassing and I felt disgusting, but I couldn't do anything back. I just froze until they left. There were other girls they would touch too.' A group of the girls complained to a teacher and the boys were spoken to and given a written punishment, but it didn't stop them. How did it affect Sarah? 'I feel really guilty and embarrassed about it all,' she says. 'It changed me – I didn't look forward to going to school.'

Concerned that sexual bullying, and its consequences, are not high enough up the government's agenda, Womankind has been running a campaign against sexual bullying in schools, and this week it published recommendations to help tackle it. There should, it says, be more teacher training and support; the issues should be dealt with across the whole school so it becomes part of the culture, not something that is just talked about in occasional personal, social and health education classes; and anti-gender bullying content should be included in classes across the curriculum.

Womankind has been involved with an education programme for three years and has held workshops in several schools; around 350 others have the lesson pack it has produced. 'At the moment, the government is putting money into tackling racial and homophobic bullying, but there is no explicit work being done on gender bullying,' says Banos Smith.

'We know schools are bombarded with initiatives,' says Hannah White, Womankind's UK schools campaign officer, who leads the workshops. 'This isn't about improving league tables, but it is linked to academic achievement. For instance, if you dispel one gender stereotype that boys are meant to be thick or muck about in lessons, then you can raise achievement.'

Mossley Hollins high school in Tameside is one of the schools at which White has held workshops. Fourteen of its older students were involved. 'There wasn't a problem with sexual bullying, but minor issues did crop up from time to time, as I'm sure they do in most schools,' says Chris Power, an English teacher and head of the upper school. 'The workshops were about raising

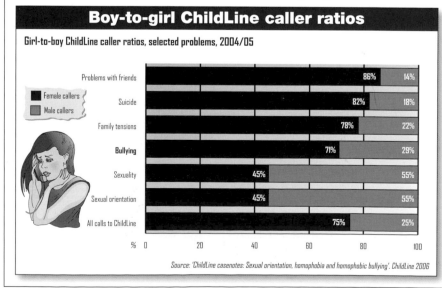

Boy-to-girl ChildLine caller ratios

Girl-to-boy ChildLine caller ratios, selected problems, 2004/05

	Female callers	Male callers
Problems with friends	86%	14%
Suicide	82%	18%
Family tensions	78%	22%
Bullying	71%	29%
Sexuality	45%	55%
Sexual orientation	45%	55%
All calls to ChildLine	75%	25%

% 0   20   40   60   80   100

Source: 'ChildLine casenotes: Sexual orientation, homophobia and homophobic bullying'. ChildLine 2006

awareness, not just in school but for the students when they go out into the workplace and in later life.'

What has been most effective, she says, is that the students who took part delivered a lesson to younger students, and have been involved in 'counselling' sessions with boys where instances of sexual bullying have cropped up – once when a 14-year-old boy pulled at a girl's skirt in PE (he was also punished), another time when a 12-year-old girl was upset because a boy had been harassing her because he wanted to go out with her. 'They need to be informed and made aware about why these things are not acceptable, and the students respond well to their peers educating them about these issues,' says Power.

'I learned a lot,' says Claire Morris, 15, who took part in the workshop. 'Even by talking about things like domestic violence, which might affect us when we're older.'

The group made a list of school rules, which included, for example, the fact that calling someone 'gay' as an insult was unacceptable, as was harassment and inappropriate touching. The boys found it equally useful. 'Boys don't know how to talk to girls,' says James Wilcock, 16. 'They'll try and impress girls, or try to look hard in front of their mates. I think this has made boys more aware and made them see that they don't have to do what their friends do.'

A survey for the National Union of Teachers showed that half of teachers had witnessed sexist language and bullying, and that, where it occurs, it occurs frequently. In America, where much more research has been done on sexual harassment in schools, a study by the American Association of University Women found that four out of five girls and boys (because it affects boys too, especially boys who are, or are perceived to be, gay) had suffered sexual bullying at some point.

The consequences of sexual bullying in schools may go much further than the distress it causes at the time. 'Schools may serve as the training grounds for domestic violence and sexual assault through the public performance of sexual harassment and gender violence,' says Nan Stein, a research scientist at the US research institute Wellesley Centers for Women, who has spent many years examining sexual harassment in schools in the US. 'It is frightening because if it is allowed to go on in public, it is as if it gives permission to proceed. You don't grow out of [sexual harassment], you grow into it, whereas a lot of bullying behaviours, such as exclusion, cease as kids get older.' In the US at least, Stein believes sexual harassment in schools is increasing. 'It is getting more sexually violent and it is happening at a younger age.'

A 14-year-old girl in Essex endured months of being called a 'slag' and a 'skank' and contemplated suicide; one day about 30 teenagers set on her, pulling her top down and exposing her breasts

---

Workshops such as the one run by Womankind help, Stein thinks, but she says there needs to be wider measures, including social workers and counselling services in schools and greater parental engagement. She believes that students' social and emotional development should be taken as seriously as their academic achievement.

Anecdotally, sexual bullying in the UK seems to be on the rise. Gemma Lang, 22, was the victim of bullies when she was at school and now runs a support group. She says she has started to hear more about sexual bullying. 'I have had girls tell me that boys will stick their hands up their skirts,' she says. 'Boys will talk to girls like dirt, and spread rumours about them being promiscuous. That didn't happen to the same extent when I was at school, it's a concept of bullying that is new to me.'

Alex Brewer, a secondary school teacher, taught until recently at a large comprehensive school in London and witnessed sexual bullying on many occasions. 'You could see it particularly among year eight and nine boys [those aged 12 to 14], who would make lewd references to girls,' he says. 'It is a form of testing out their masculinity, but in a horrible way, and they usually picked on vulnerable girls. They would grab their crotches in front of the girls. You felt it was an intimidating atmosphere. I've seen boys put up pornography from the Internet in computer lessons and leave it on the screen as a way to intimidate girls and other boys.'

What is the effect on the girls? 'I think it affects all the children,' says Brewer. 'Girls will play up to sexual stereotypes to defend themselves – they will pretend to know what a blowjob is or boast about it, and this can be damaging to them.' It can also lead to girls not living up to their academic potential. 'It makes girls shut down in class. They will not answer questions or give a talk to a class if they are attacked by boys – even if that attack is just winks or jeers.'
30 November 2007
© *Guardian Newspapers Limited 2008*

An inclusive culture

Challenging homophobic and sexist bullying

A harmless joke? A trivial matter? Boys being boys? If the card had been assigned a racist term, would we think differently about this incident?

Half of all teachers do not challenge homophobic language when they hear it. The reasons for this are varied, but combined they contribute to a wide ranging conspiracy of silence. As a result, homophobia remains a pervasive and persistent problem within our society, including in our schools and colleges.

In July this year, the charity Stonewall published *The School Report*, which documents the experiences of over 1,100 lesbian, gay and bisexual pupils in Britain's schools. The report notes that almost two-thirds of young lesbian, gay and bisexual (LGB) pupils at secondary school have experienced homophobic bullying.

ATL believes that homophobia and homophobic bullying affect everyone. It is part of a wider culture that encourages particular stereotypes of men and women. In order to challenge homophobia and homophobic bullying, we must therefore also tackle the underlying stereotypes.

'Doing gender': cultural stereotypes of masculinity and femininity

Being 'popular' and 'fitting in' by taking up the dominant positions of masculinity and femininity are expressed by pupils as extremely important. Homophobia and sexism are key elements in this process of 'doing gender', which is generally defined as conforming to and behaving in line with prevailing constructions of masculine and

the education union

feminine identities. Various studies have, for example, commented on the powerful role of homophobia within male peer culture and in constructing and reinforcing stereotypical ideas of what it means to be a 'real' boy or man.

Based on the assumption of heterosexuality, boys who define themselves as masculine subjects in conformity with this dominant masculinity tend to position themselves in opposition to girls/women, gay or bisexual and/or non-macho boys/men. For girls, a socially acceptable femininity is also premised on the norm of heterosexuality, and includes a requirement to have a 'feminine' appearance, thus marking girls out as different to the boys.

Deviations from these 'feminine' conventions, including being too sexual, too popular, too different or too confident, are thereby stigmatised as being evidence of a girl's 'distorted' sexuality and expressed, for example, in pejorative comments about the girl being 'butch', a 'slag', a 'bitch', or a 'lezzie'. Boys' and girls' sex/gender identities are developed under constant pressure and surveillance between and within male and female peer groups. In the classroom, boys frequently silence girls through sexist abuse and sexual harassment. At the same time, homophobia serves as a means for boys to distance themselves from femininity and forcefully reject boys who do not conform to the dominant standard of masculinity.

The emphasis on heterosexuality thereby ensures that the story of 'romance', which promotes male dominance and female subordination, is not challenged or dislocated by girls who, within the context of their own heterosexuality, might display more 'laddish' behaviours. Although there are alternative forms of masculinity and femininity in our culture that, in some manifestations, challenge the cultural stereotypes, they are usually posited as 'deviant' and therefore remain subordinate to the dominant cultural expectations of masculinity and femininity.

ATL recognises that teachers and lecturers have an important role in addressing and challenging

such prejudices and stereotypes, including through the school/college's ethos and mission statement, the curriculum, pastoral support systems, working with parents, governors and the community, and through specific initiatives such as the celebration of LGBT History Month or International Women's Day.

Every child matters and youth matters

Narrow and stereotypical views of male and female identity restrict all boys and girls. They restrict not only the victims of homophobic and/or sexist bullying and abuse, who are disproportionately more likely to truant, drop out of school without any qualifications and are at an increased risk to self-harm and/or commit suicide, but they also restrict those individuals who fear social isolation and bullying and thus feel under pressure to prove their 'masculinity' or 'femininity' by engaging in abusive or risk-taking behaviour.

The Education and Inspections Act 2006 requires schools and colleges to implement measures that encourage respect for others, promote self-discipline amongst pupils, and prevent all forms of bullying, including homophobic and sexist bullying. Schools and colleges also have a responsibility under the Government's Every Child Matters agenda to ensure that 'every child and young person is able to fulfil their potential'. This means that schools and colleges must systematically and consistently deal with specific homophobic and sexist incidents and

should simultaneously begin to tackle the underlying culture leading to homophobic and sexist behaviour.

ATL believes that the need for a wider process of cultural change requires a more in-depth understanding of the interrelatedness of homophobia and sexism.

Why do we need a focus on homophobia and sexism?

There are at least three reasons to suggest a focus on homophobia and sexism as interrelated manifestations of a culture that privileges particular stereotypes of masculinity and femininity.

Sexist bullying is not just perpetrated by boys or men

Sexist bullying is predominantly perpetrated by males upon females. Girls and young women are almost twice as likely to be on the child protection register for sexual abuse as boys and young men. Statistics also show that in the UK, two women per week are killed by a male partner or former partner, and that one in four women will be a victim of domestic violence in their lifetime.

However, the Anti-Bullying Alliance notes that sexist bullying has 'an impact on both genders, and can be perpetrated by both genders on opposite and same-gender victims'. The concept of sexism alone is not inclusive enough to facilitate such an awareness. In particular, the sexist bullying of girls by other girls as part of establishing conformity to dominant expectations of femininity and to the related boundaries of appropriate sexuality and sexual behaviour is not readily associated with the term sexism.

Homophobic bullying is not restricted to lesbian, gay and bisexual people

Homophobic bullying and abuse is not exclusively targeted at lesbian, gay and bisexual people, but also at those who are perceived to be lesbian, gay or bisexual, or who do not conform to existing sex/gender codes. The term 'homophobia', which is generally defined as the passive or active resentment or fear of someone who is lesbian, gay or bisexual, does not

explicitly include a reference to a lack of conformity to stereotypical notions of masculinity and femininity.

Although homophobia presupposes such stereotypes by identifying behaviour that 'deviates' from these cultural norms as 'gay', we might wish to resist the homophobic notion of the existence of 'gay behaviour'.

Homophobic abuse of gay men frequently involves language that is derogatory to females

The vocabulary of homophobic abuse of gay males commonly consists of terms derogatory to females, such as 'sissy', 'girl', 'faggot', and 'nancy boy'. This interrelatedness of homophobia and sexism is also expressed in the regular and wholly pejorative use of the term 'effeminate' to identify a 'lack' of masculinity in boys or men and at the same time stigmatise the 'effete' or 'effeminate' male through the term's simultaneous association with homosexuality.

Tackling homophobia and sexism using the concept of heterosexism

The concept of heterosexism includes a focus on both homophobia and sexism and therefore enables us to account for the underlying cultural prejudice against lesbian, gay and bisexual people. This prejudice is firmly tied to dominant male and female identities that rely on heterosexuality as a norm. Heterosexism includes attitudes, behaviour and practices that constitute heterosexuality as the norm. At the same time, heterosexism reflects and encourages a dislike or feeling of superiority towards girls and women.

ATL believes that we can only successfully tackle sexism and homophobia by seeing them as two integral parts of the wider cultural problem of heterosexism. Heterosexism advocates and supports a narrowly defined set of heterosexual sex/gender identities that restrict everyone. Those who do not conform to these stereotypical notions of 'masculinity' and 'femininity' are frequently subjected to homophobic and sexist bullying and abuse.

ATL therefore recommends that heterosexism is widely adopted as the concept through which we challenge the narrow and restrictive stereotypes of masculinity and femininity as well as understanding the close links between homophobia and sexism. Tackling homophobic and sexist bullying and abuse using the concept of heterosexism means that our educational institutions will be better equipped to contribute to a change in social attitudes and the promotion of a more inclusive, equitable and just society in which everyone, regardless of their sex/gender identity and sexual orientation, feels equally valued, respected and safe.

This position statement is based on existing research and educational thinking around these issues in the UK and elsewhere.

Terminology

Gender generally refers to the social and cultural constructions of masculinity and femininity and indicates that a man or woman's position is not dictated by nature, biology or sex, but is a matter of social and political convention.

Sex refers more specifically to male or female physiology as biological constructions of the body.

In this document, we have used the term sex/gender to indicate that even the depiction of male and female physiognomy has depended on the social and political significance accorded to gendered notions of masculinity and femininity. Physiological difference as the 'natural' basis for gender difference therefore cannot be separated from social and cultural constructions of manhood and womanhood.

Sexist bullying includes abusive name-calling; gestures and comments about appearance and emerging puberty; sexual innuendos and propositions; the public display of pornographic material and graffiti with sexual content; domestic or intimate abuse; and sexual assault or rape. Most commonly, sexist bullying is perpetrated by males upon females and is based on a dislike of or feeling of superiority towards girls and women. Women are thereby seen as legitimate targets for sexist and sexualised behaviour.

Homophobic bullying is often present in an environment that fails to challenge and respond to homophobia. It can be verbal, which involves name-calling, public ridicule, text messaging and the regular use of offensive and discriminatory language that refers to someone's sexual orientation. It also often manifests itself indirectly through the spreading of rumours and/or the social isolation of the individual. In its most severe form, homophobic bullying is characterised by physical attacks and sexual assault.

Homophobic bullying does not just affect people who identify as LGBT. In schools, homophobic bullying can directly affect any young person whose life choices, interests or needs do not conform to accepted gender norms, as well as adult members of the school community who are LGBT, and anyone who may have friends or relatives who are LGBT (DfES, *Stand Up for Us*, 2004).

⇨ The above information is reprinted with kind permission from ATL, the education union. Visit www.atl.org.uk for more information.

© ATL

Bullying wrecks lives

The experiences of children and young people with a learning disability

Nearly all children and young people with a learning disability are bullied

Ashley's story

'I'm still scared of the bullies and I'm worried walking alone in school, in case I bump into him.'

I'm Ashley and I'm 12 years old. I like to play computer games and to go on the Internet. I want to design

computer games and animations. I need help with reading and writing.

On the first day I started my new school, I was told by a bully to get out of his school. He said he did not like the look of me. He had two more bully friends – a boy and girl. I was spat on, sweared at and kicked.

I came home moody and upset, I did not want to go back to school. I hated the bully and his friends.

8 out of 10 children with a learning disability are bullied

82% of children and young people with a learning disability have experienced bullying. They are twice as likely to be bullied as other children.[1]

Children with a learning disability are more likely to be targeted by bullies because of their disability. They are seen as 'different'. They

may be doing different work at school, or they may find it hard to make friends or join in play activities. Other children can see them as 'easy targets' because they can be made to get into trouble, or because they may not understand that what is happening to them is bullying.[2]

Like racist and homophobic bullying, disablist bullying is particularly harmful as it is based on prejudice. Bullying of children with a learning disability discriminates against children who find it hard to understand bullying, to tell people about it, and to be listened to and supported. It damages children's self-esteem and has a huge impact on the way children and young people with a learning disability see themselves.

'Alice has been taunted with "Alice's brother is a spac, Alice's brother goes uh, uh, uh".'

Children with a learning disability are bullied wherever they go

So far, the focus of most research on bullying has been on schools. 8 out of 10 children and young people with a learning disability who have been bullied had experienced bullying at school. But Mencap's research reveals that children with a learning disability are being bullied everywhere they go.

82% of young people with a learning disability have experienced bullying. They are twice as likely to be bullied as other children

---

3 out of 10 children and young people with a learning disability who have been bullied were bullied out on the street, with the same number experiencing bullying at the park and on the bus. Children also reported being bullied at youth clubs and in leisure centres.

5 out of 10 children with a learning disability had been bullied in more than one place. Children with a learning disability already face barriers in accessing education and leisure opportunities – bullying compounds this, preventing them from living full and happy lives.

'People call me names on the street.'

6 out of 10 children with a learning disability are physically hurt by bullies

It is shocking that so many children with a learning disability are being subjected to physical forms of bullying in their neighbourhoods. This includes children being punched and slapped, spat on, knocked over, and, in some cases, attacked with such violence that hospital treatment is needed.

In many cases the physical bullying that children and young people with a learning disability experience should be classified and treated as assault or abuse. Yet these attacks are rarely subject to police investigation, and also not afforded the protection of safeguarding procedures.[3]

Physical attacks on children and young people with a learning disability are never acceptable, and must be treated extremely seriously.

'I had to be taken to hospital to have 18 stitches in my forehead.'

Intimidation and other abuse hurts too

77% of children and young people with a learning disability are verbally abused. Calling a child with a learning disability hurtful and insulting names related to their disability is discriminatory behaviour, and a particularly insidious form of bullying.

Bullies also target children with a learning disability by taking their things or leaving them out of activities – 4 out of 10 children with a learning disability said this had happened to them.

Bullying in all its forms needs to be recognised, prevented and dealt with seriously.

'When I was being bullied I was very upset. I tried to hide how I felt. It was hard.'

Bullying wrecks the lives of children and young people with a learning disability

Ben's story

'We had to move. The bullying had become so severe that Ben would no longer leave the house.'

Ben, who has Down's syndrome, was just 15 when his life was ruined by bullies.

'When we moved house, Ben was desperate to make friends with the local children,' explains his mum, Charlotte. 'But he often returned home with spit on him or the tyres of his bike deflated. On some days he was chased by a group of children until he reached the safety of home.'

Ben couldn't understand why the other children didn't want to be his friend. His mum found it very hard to tell him that they saw him as different because of his Down's syndrome. She was afraid that this would make him feel frustrated about his learning disability.

Charlotte says: 'Ben was bullied wherever he went. He would return from the park with bruises and torn clothes. As far as the local kids were concerned, Ben was there for their entertainment. He was the butt of their jokes, an object to ridicule.'

The ongoing bullying left Ben terrified to go outside. Having previously been an independent young man, he began to have recurring nightmares, and refused to leave the house. Whenever he heard children's voices outside he would cower and beg his mum not to let them near him.

Last year Ben and his mum moved to a new home in a different area. Ben, now 19, is receiving counselling to help him deal with the ongoing distress that the bullying has caused. He is much happier. Nonetheless, he is still very upset about what happened to him and refuses to go anywhere near his old home.

8 out of 10 children with a learning disability are scared to go out

Children with a learning disability are scared to leave their homes because of bullying. They are most afraid to go to school, the park and out on the street.

Over half of children with a learning disability who have been bullied stopped going to the places where the bullying happened. These children already face significant barriers in our society. It is far harder for them to access opportunities to learn and achieve. Bullying is another barrier that prevents them from taking part in their communities and doing the things others might take for granted.

Some children with a learning disability have been forced to change schools to escape bullying. This is extremely disruptive to their education. The solution to bullying should not be to force the child who has been bullied to leave.

All children have the right to feel safe in their communities. Disabled children also have the right to live their lives free from discrimination and harassment.[4] But this right is simply not the reality for thousands of children and young people with a learning disability.

'I don't like the street, I don't like the park, I don't like the swimming pool because of bullies.'

Bullying damages self-esteem

Many children and young people with a learning disability have low self-esteem. Being taunted, intimidated and abused because of their disability damages their sense of self-worth.

Children with a learning disability often find it harder to make friends than other children, so being bullied leaves them feeling lonely and depressed. 56% of children with a learning disability said they cried because of bullying, and 33% hid away in their bedroom.

'Bullying makes me feel sad.'

Bullying does not stop

Peter's story*

'I told my teachers at school and they said that I had special needs so I should get used to it as I would be bullied all my life.'

I'm Peter and I'm 17 years old. In my spare time I like horse riding and playing on my computer.

When I went to my old school I got bullied really badly. I got bullied at break times by other children at school. They would call me names, spit at me and throw stones and bottles at me.

The bullying made me feel very angry and sad. The bullying stopped me going out at home, so I lost all my mates. I don't have any mates any more, so I don't play out any more.

I told my teachers at school and they said that I had special needs so I should get used to it as I would be bullied all my life. They also told me to stop playing out at break times then I would not get bullied.

The bullying carried on until my mum and dad found out and then I moved schools.

I want adults to stop the bullies. And I want people to listen to us when we tell them what's happening.

*Not his real name.

Bullying did not stop for 4 out of 10 children when they told someone

Children and young people with a learning disability most commonly told a teacher or a parent that they were being bullied. However, for 4 out of 10 children who told someone, the bullying did not stop. This confirms the conclusions of the National Autistic Society's 'B is for Bullying' report (2006), which found that in 44% of cases, no action was taken by the school after it was reported that a child with autism was being bullied.

Adults do not always believe children with a learning disability when they report bullying, or they don't treat it is a serious matter. If an adult dismisses a child's reports or tells them that bullying is just part of life, they are condoning disablist bullying. All adults who work with children need to know how to deal with disablist bullying appropriately. And they must ensure that it is always treated seriously.

'The girls were nasty, they told lies. No one believed me.'

Children with a learning disability find it hard to report bullying

Sometimes when a child with a learning disability is being bullied they do not understand what is happening. They think that being treated badly is just a part of their everyday life. Others find it hard to give a clear account of what has happened to them, which can lead to their reports of bullying not being acted upon.

Signs that a child with a learning disability is being bullied can often be missed. For example, a child with a learning disability could show a change in behaviour because they are distressed about being bullied.

Adults could simply attribute the change to the child's disability and therefore dismiss it.[5] Adults should be aware of children and young people with a learning disability who are at risk of being bullied. They should take preventative steps, followed by firm action if they see or suspect bullying.

'I don't like being bullied. It does not stop when I tell someone.'

Many children with a learning disability are bullied throughout their lives

Nearly half of children with a learning disability had been bullied for over a year, and many were bullied for even longer. Children with a learning disability are being bullied for a significant period of their childhood, which has a hugely negative impact on their development and life chances.

The effects of bullying in childhood can still be felt by people with a learning disability when they become adults. When children with a learning disability are denied opportunities to learn, develop and achieve because of bullying, they find it harder to develop their skills and confidence in adult life. This then makes it more likely that they will also be targets for abuse as adults.

Many adults with a learning disability are bullied in their communities, as Mencap's *Living in Fear* report[6] revealed. Disablist bullying can escalate into the abuse, hate crime, and even murder of adults with a learning disability.[7]

'It is horrible being bullied. It needs to stop.'

Notes

1 Compared to research findings in 'Tackling Bullying: Listening to the views of children and young people in schools', Department for Education and Skills 2003.

2 *They won't believe me*, Mencap, 2005 (www.mencap.org.uk/html/campaigns/anti_bullying/more_info.asp)

3 The School Standards and Framework Act (1999) and the Education Act (2002) both place a legal obligation on schools to promote and safeguard the welfare of children and to prevent bullying.

4 Disability Discrimination Acts, 1995 and 2005.

5 *They won't believe me*, Mencap, 2005.

6 *Living in Fear*, Mencap, 1999.

7 In one case, three people were jailed for the murder of a man with a learning disability who the judge said was literally 'bullied to death' in 2007.

November 2007

⇨ The above information is reprinted with kind permission from Mencap. Visit www.mencap.org.uk for more information.

© *Mencap*

Truths we must face up to

Kira Cochrane is outraged by the bullying of the disabled

I tend not to have much time for those hell-in-a-handcart folk who claim society is worse than it's ever been, that we've lost our values, are beset by crime, are slowly turning 'feral'. My suspicion has always been – while more explicit news reporting might have upped our fears – that society doesn't change that much in its basic balance of cruelty and kindness.

Recently, though, a string of crimes has almost made me believe we are, indeed, going to the dogs. Bullying and violence against the disabled seems to have reached such horrific levels that claims of our turning feral no longer sound so far-fetched. Take the case of Christine Lakinski, a 50-year-old with a spine deformity, who had suffered bullying throughout her life. Back in July, Lakinski fell over and lay dying in the street near her house – at which point she might have expected help from her neighbours. Instead, Anthony Anderson, 27, emerged from his house and was joined by friends. He first kicked Lakinski and then urinated on her.

Then there was the case of Fiona Ann Pilkington, 38, whose daughter, Francesca Hardwick, 18, had severe learning disabilities. Two weeks ago, Pilkington is thought to have murdered her daughter and killed herself by setting fire to the car they were in, after they suffered a sustained campaign of abuse from local children. (She had complained about this repeatedly to the police.) The harassment apparently included children standing outside the family home shouting 'disabled bitch' and throwing stones and eggs at the windows.

There have been other deaths. March 2006: Keith Philpott, who had learning difficulties, was tortured to death at his flat in Teesside. July 2006: Steven Hoskin, a man with severe learning difficulties, was targeted by a group who cheated him out of his benefits, dragged him around his bedsit on a dog lead, before forcing him to take 70 painkillers and pushing him over the safety rail of a railway viaduct. Hoskin held on with his fingertips. One of the group stamped on his hands.

Still reading? I wouldn't blame you if you'd stopped. It may be unprofessional to admit it, but, hell, reading through the cuttings for this column I found myself crying uncontrollably.

There is more. September 2006: Kevin Davies, who suffered from epilepsy, was imprisoned in a shed for four months by his 'friends', beaten daily, starved, burned, before a beating that ended in his death. August 2007: Brent Martin, who had learning difficulties, was stripped and beaten in the street, his injuries so severe that his uncle – outside whose home he finally collapsed – didn't recognise him when he went to his aid. Martin died in hospital.

The bullying of the disabled is endemic: in 1999, a survey by Mencap found that nine out of ten people with learning difficulties had been bullied. Earlier this year, a survey by the same charity found that eight out of ten children with a learning disability had been bullied, with the same proportion too scared to go out.

What can be done? An obvious answer is that social services must ensure those with learning disabilities receive the help they need – whether they live independently or with a carer. In Steven Hoskin's case, he had begun living away from his mother for the first time in his mid-thirties, receiving regular visits from Cornwall's department for adult social care until a month before his death. When contact ceased, the abuse he had suffered for months proved fatal.

Questions have been asked about whether the police response to Fiona Ann Pilkington's complaints of harassment was good enough (a police spokeswoman has described such suggestions as 'unfair'). Whatever the truth in that case, it is clearly of the utmost importance that police respond swiftly and appropriately to such complaints. In 2003, there was some forward movement within the judicial system, when crimes motivated by a victim's disability were recognised as a form of hate crime.

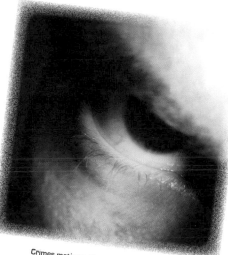

Crimes motivated by a victim's disability are recognised as a form of hate crime

As a result, those convicted of such offences can be given a higher tariff. But, as Ruth Scott, head of policy at Scope, has pointed out, the crimes against Hoskin and Davies were never actually investigated to see if disability hate crime was an aggravating factor.

Steps can be taken to tackle this bullying and violence, but there will never be improvements unless, as a society, we tap into our natural outrage. When murders motivated by racism or homophobia occur, there is, rightly, a public outcry – a recognition that if some good can be culled from the situation it is the reminder that such prejudice needs to be dealt with.

I understand why people look away from such stories. They feel too medieval, too feral, to confront. But until we express our outrage, we all inhabit a small corner of complicity.
8 November 2007

↪ The above information is reprinted with kind permission from the *New Statesman*. Visit www.newstatesman. com for more information.
© *New Statesman*

70% of kids are bullies

Information from Beatbullying

More than seven in 10 children have been a bully, shocking new figures from Beatbullying reveal.

56% of young people have experienced bullying, but new figures show that over 70% of young people have bullied, quashing the notion of a small minority of bullies wielding power over a majority of victims.

The research, conducted across a nationally representative sample of 3,000 secondary school-aged young people, was carried out by Beatbullying's research team on the ground from 2005 to 2007.

The findings give, for the first time, an insight into the scope of the bullying problem from a new perspective. In an effort to understand the motivations of a bully, Beatbullying asked young people if they had ever bullied and if so, what had led them to do it.

Of these bullies, 5% said if they didn't do it first it would happen to them, 4% said that they bully because their mates do it, 13% said anger was the reason and amazingly just over 2% thought it made them popular.

Emma-Jane Cross, Chief Executive of Beatbullying, said:

'These figures show that the majority of bullying taking place in schools is not perpetrated by a recitative minority. Most bullying is low-level, perpetrated by young people who are easily led or incorrectly believe that it is inevitable, or worst still, that it makes them popular. The good news is that these young people are within our grasp, they are not the hard to reach with severe behavioural problems. Beatbullying can continue to educate these young people to easily change their behaviour.

'The other interesting finding of this research is that 13% of bullies do so because they are angry. Why is anger leading so many young people to take it out on each other? What are they angry about? A lot more work needs to be done here.

'For us to prevent bullying properly it is necessary to understand why young people bully in the first place. We believe bullies must be part of the solution, we must educate them as part of the wider community so they can make the decision to stop bullying.'

For Beatbullying, this approach works. Their research shows that, after being through the Beatbullying peer mentoring programmes (or BB Mentors), 77% of young people who had bullied in the past said that Beatbullying had helped them stop bullying and changed their attitude towards bullying.

Ms Cross continued:

'What is most surprising for us is that after all the successful campaigns to highlight the nasty effects of bullying, we are still finding that 2% of bullies do it because they think it makes them popular. 2% may seem tiny, but that's about 60,000 bullies out there doing it because they think it makes them popular! We need to reach these young people swiftly and decisively.'

Perhaps most successfully, 92% of young graduates from BB Mentors who had been bullied in the past reported that they were no longer being bullied. Proving that Beatbullying's prevention approach has a 360 degree success rate – helping both the bullies to stop bullying and the bullied to prevent bullying happening to them.

Beatbullying believes that bullying contradicts the basic British values of fair play, of social justice, of aspiration, of opportunity, of respect – it is something the whole nation must act collectively to eradicate, so we can support the millions of young people who lie in bed at night terrified to go to school the next morning. Young people that are being bullied at school are not able to make the most of themselves and their talents, because their ability to learn, to contribute, to be happy and just be a child is undermined and sometimes lost for ever by bullying. The introduction of progressive bullying prevention programmes in the UK will reduce bullying, reduce truancy levels, increase attainment and reduce the incidents of racist and homophobic violence and abuse in our schools. In the best cases the BB Mentors programme has reduced bullying in schools by 80%.

Snapshot of the findings

71.4% said they had bullied someone, of these:

⇨ 13% admitted anger was the reason.

⇨ 10% were bullied themselves.

⇨ 5% said if they didn't do it first, it would happen to them.

⇨ 4% stated their mates do it.

⇨ 2% thought it made them popular.

25 February 2008

⇨ The above information is reprinted with kind permission from Beatbullying. Visit www.beatbullying.org for more information.

© Beatbullying

Are you a bully?

Information from BullyingUK

Around 16 pupils in the UK kill themselves every year due to distress over bullying.

Their schools often say they had no idea what was going on. But the bullies know exactly what they've been doing – and so do their friends. It's too late to have regrets when someone has died, or been made so ill they need medical treatment.

You're a bully if you do any of these things to someone else:

⇨ You call them names.
⇨ You make up stories to get them into trouble.
⇨ You tell other people not to be friends with them.
⇨ You make remarks about their culture, religion or colour.
⇨ You make remarks about their disability or medical condition.
⇨ You leave them out when you're choosing a games team.
⇨ You take away their possessions or demand money from them.
⇨ You hide their books or bag.
⇨ You send them nasty text messages or make silent calls to their phone.
⇨ You make threats about nasty things that will happen to them.
⇨ You make remarks about them liking other boys or other girls. This is called homophobic bullying.
⇨ You spread rumours about them.
⇨ You take their friends away leaving them on their own.

⇨ You hit them, kick them, trip them up or push them around.
⇨ You make remarks about their looks or weight.
⇨ You don't choose them to be your partner in class.
⇨ You tell them you're busy and then go off to enjoy yourself with other people.
⇨ You damage their property.
⇨ You make jokes about them when you can see they're upset.
⇨ You indulge in horseplay when you know they are not enjoying it.
⇨ You're going along with the crowd who are doing any of these thing.

Bullying can make people feel really upset and depressed

Here is what some pupils told us in just one week:

'She has taken all my friends away and I go home at night and I'm depressed and cry' – girl aged 13
'One time I wouldn't eat because of people calling me "fat"' – boy aged 14
'Mondays were worst because I had to face the bully again and I soon got so worried it made me ill' – teenage girl
'I feel lonely and I want some advice about how to feel better about myself, going to school' – girl aged 15
'I feel like killing myself, it's that bad. I will probably end up in hospital, I have no friends and if I don't get help now I will end up a mess' – girl aged 14

'Other kids trip me up and call me names. It got so bad once that I ran away from school' – boy aged 12
'They stir things up so people don't want to be my friend. I'm depressed, annoyed, stressed and keep breaking down in tears. I feel like I'm about to fall apart' – boy aged 13
'I pray to make the bullies better people but it really upsets me because none of my friends stick up for me. They just sit there and laugh' – teenage girl

Risks you run if you bully someone else

You run quite a few risks if you bully someone else. You could get a warning, detention, temporary or permanent exclusion (expulsion). A violent, one-off incident harming another pupil could be grounds for expulsion.

Around 16 pupils in the UK kill themselves every year due to distress over bullying

If an incident involves violence, text phone, Internet abuse or demands for money then the victim and their parents should, and probably will, make a complaint to the police.

If you are over the age of criminal responsibility, which is 10 in England and Wales, you could be charged with assault or harassment. Even if the case doesn't go to court but results in a caution that could still have a serious effect on your future.

If you bully someone out of school the council or police could apply for an anti-social behaviour order (ASBO).

Bullies think that if they use false names on the Internet they can get away with it but they can't. See the Internet section on the BullyingUK website (www.bullying.co.uk) for information about that.

Some young people have been so upset they've killed themselves

There have been many cases where teenagers have killed themselves due to bullying and no doubt the bullies never thought this would be the consequence.

Bullying UK gets hundreds of emails a month and a surprising proportion are from secondary school pupils who say they are suicidal now or have been in the past. Some have been cutting themselves due to their distress. Others are receiving psychiatric and psychological help. Many of them are too frightened to go to school and some have been removed from school by their parents.

If you bully someone out of school the council or police could apply for an anti-social behaviour order (ASBO)

We also get emails from pupils suffering from eating disorders because they have been called fat when they are perfectly normal, and others from pupils with Asperger's syndrome who are teased because their condition makes it difficult to relate to other people.

Bullies also target those who are more clever, more popular and better looking than they are as well as those who stand out in any way perhaps because they wear spectacles, have red hair, dyslexia, diabetes or are just quiet and pleasant.

If you're bullying someone else do you really want to be responsible for another person having a mental breakdown and suffering unhappiness that can last a lifetime?

Contact us on help@bullying.co.uk if you need more help.

⇨ The above information is reprinted with kind permission from BullyingUK. Visit www.bullying.co.uk for more information.
© BullyingUK

Study looks at why the bullies carry on bullying

Young male bullies are aware of the damage that they cause their victims but carry on to guarantee their own personal gain, according to findings of preliminary research at the University of Sussex

Developmental psychologists David Smalley (a DPhil student) and Dr Robin Banerjee presented the findings of their research at the recent annual conference of the British Psychological Society's Developmental Section in Plymouth.

Previous research has shown that bullies tend to be aware of the damage that their behaviour has on their victims. This study investigates why they continue to victimise their peers despite this understanding.

Fifty-five children aged seven to nine were assessed on their social understanding of specific social situations and then scored for bullying/victimisation.

The study found that bullying by both boys and girls could occur despite the fact that they understand the feelings of the person they are bullying. In particular, the results showed that male bullies had a general tendency to focus on their own personal gain in these situations.

Mr Smalley says: 'Previous research has found that bullies may have mature social understanding and therefore know the upset and damage that they cause to their victims. We are now investigating why they continue with this behaviour.

'Findings of this preliminary research suggest that bullies may have different goals in social situations compared with other children, focusing especially on self-gain.

'By studying the way bullies reconcile their awareness of the harm they do, we hope to be able to help anti-bullying initiatives understand this behaviour – and benefit bullies and victims alike.'

Further research will consist of a far larger study of 200 or so children and will consider more specific measures of empathic ability in order to test this hypothesis.

13 September 2007

⇨ The above information is reprinted with kind permission from the University of Sussex. Visit www.sussex.ac.uk for more information.
© *University of Sussex*

What is a bully?

Stereotypical image of school bully needs updating, researchers say

The stereotypical image of the school bully needs to be revised, researchers at the Institute of Education, London, have concluded.

Less than 1 per cent of primary school children are 'true bullies', and most children who bully are themselves bullied by other pupils, the researchers say. Bullies are also more likely than their classmates to suffer from low self-esteem, depression, and behavioural problems from early childhood and through primary school. They are more likely to suffer from mental health problems later in life too.

Dr Leslie Gutman, lead author of the new study, believes that schools need to teach that bullying is unacceptable and hold bullies to account for their actions. However, she feels that there should also be greater awareness of the wider possible consequences and causes of bullying behaviour.

The study by the Centre for Research on the Wider Benefits of Learning (WBL) found that 75 per cent of children enjoy healthy friendships. But the one in four who does not may often have suffered from issues such as language delays, conduct problems, and hyperactivity from an early age.

The report highlights the value of existing government initiatives, such as peer mentoring, the Social and Emotional Aspects of Learning programme, and national strategies for targeting schools with bullying issues. However, Dr Gutman, Research Director at WBL, says: 'Early interventions that teach children coping strategies for developmental difficulties such as hyperactivity may also alleviate the later possibility of being targeted as victims and/or engaging in bullying.

'We are not suggesting that schools should adopt a soft approach to bullying but simply stating that, on the basis of the evidence, bullying is a more complex issue than some people believe it to be.'

The researchers used data from the Avon Longitudinal Study of Parents and Children to study 6,500 pupils aged 8 to 11. They also found that children with happier friendships are more likely to have married parents and more educated mothers. Girls are more likely than boys to have larger numbers of friends, while boys are more likely to be both bullies and victims.

Even those who had friendships with which they were happy could have problems: in particular, children who had friendships which were otherwise supportive, but characterised by a high degree of conflict, tended to feel less in control of their lives.

The importance of social worlds: an investigation of peer relationships Wider Benefits of Learning Report No 29 can be found at http://www.learningbenefits.net/Publications/ResRepIntros/ResRep29intro.htm *28 August 2008*

↳ The above information is reprinted with kind permission from the Institute of Education, University of London. Visit www.ioe.ac.uk for more information.
© *Institute of Education, University of London*

Bullies, victims more likely to consider suicide

Information from Reuters Health

Victims of bullying – and the bullies themselves – are at increased risk of suicidal thinking and are also more likely to attempt suicide than their peers who aren't involved in bullying, according to a systematic review of 37 studies conducted in 16 different countries.

And those who were both bullies and victims were at greatest risk, Dr Young Shin Kim of Yale University School of Medicine in New Haven, Connecticut, and Dr Bennett Leventhal of the University of Illinois College of Medicine in Chicago found.

'It is imperative that there now be a common goal to intervene actively to reduce bullying in all communities and to seek out both victims and perpetrators to protect them from suicidality and other potential lethal adverse consequences of this serious public health problem,' the researchers conclude in the *International Journal of Adolescent Mental Health*.

Kim and Bennett reviewed the quality of existing research examining the relationship between suicide and bullying. About three-quarters of the studies included youth in the general population, while the rest looked at special populations such as homosexual or bisexual young people, people with developmental disorders, and young people with legal problems.

Most studies of bully victims found increased risk of suicidal behaviour, with victims being up to 5.6 times more likely to have suicidal thoughts and up to 5.4 times more likely to have made suicide attempts. But bullies themselves were up to

9 times more likely than their peers in the general population to have considered suicide, while they were up to 9.9 times more likely to try suicide. Those who were both victims and perpetrators were up to 10-fold more likely to have suicidal thoughts. Some, but not all, of the studies found an increased risk for females.

Bullying also increased the likelihood of suicidal thoughts and attempts among people with learning disabilities, drug abuse, delinquent behaviour, or who were homosexual or bisexual.

'Although many adolescents may experience bullying, either as participants or observers, the observation that it is common does not imply that it is "normal" and, hence, an acceptable part of "normal development",' the researchers write. 'Indeed, the evidence from this review suggests that exposure to bullying, especially for participants, is harmful.'

SOURCE: *International Journal of Adolescent Mental Health, July 2008*
24 July 2008

⇨ Copyright 2008 Reuters. Reprinted with permission from Reuters. Reuters content is the intellectual property of Reuters or its third party content providers. Any copying, republication or redistribution or Reuters content is expressly prohibited without the prior written consent of Reuters. Reuters shall not be liable for any errors or delays in content, or for any actions taken in reliance thereon. Reuters and the Reuters Sphere Logo are registered trademarks of the Reuters group of companies around the world. For additional information about Reuters content and services, please visit Reuters website at www. reuters.com. REU-4933-MES.

© *Reuters*

The brand-name bullies

Children are highly influenced by brands and logos – ATL

Children are highly influenced by brands and logos, with 85 per cent of teachers saying the possession of fashion and branded goods is important to their pupils, according to a survey by the Association of Teachers and Lecturers (ATL).

The survey of 380 support staff, teachers and lecturers working in schools, sixth form and further education colleges around the UK showed children's desire to fit in and be like everyone else in their class and school seems to play a huge role in the items they want to own. Teachers ranked brands, friends and logos as the top three influences on what children buy – respectively rated by 93 per cent, 91 per cent, and 77 per cent of teachers as the key influences.

Worryingly 46 per cent of teachers said young people who cannot afford the fashion items or branded goods owned by their peers have been excluded, isolated or bullied as a result.

A teacher from a school in Derbyshire said: 'Goods identified with "cheap" logos become the brunt of regular name-calling and bullying. The "geek" is isolated.'

Andy Cranham, a teacher from City of Bristol College, said: 'The need to belong in groups is paramount to young learners and exclusion is something they see as the end of the world.'

Sheila Bell, who teaches in Cumbria, said: 'They need to be up-to-date,

the education union

otherwise they get left out and have low self-esteem.'

Tamsin Buckingham who teaches in a secondary school in Surrey said: 'It is often the children who you would expect to have least, e.g. family on benefits, who have all the branded stuff and tease others.'

The influence of advertising and marketing on children is believed to be far more significant than five years ago according to 40 per cent of teachers, with 73 per cent saying it has increased on ten years ago. Teachers overwhelmingly believe – 98 per cent – that advertising directly targets children and young people.

So it is unsurprising that teachers believe children and young people exert a considerable influence on their parents' buying decisions – with 64 per cent saying children have a considerable influence on the purchase of food, branded goods, entertainment and holidays.

A teacher from a secondary school in Kent said: 'Parents give in to children's demands far more readily... this is fuelled by advertising.'

Ann Seddon, from Manor Field Infant School in Hampshire, said: 'A lot of advertising companies blatantly target children without any consideration for the parents of those children.'

Dr Mary Bousted, general secretary of the Association of Teachers and Lecturers (ATL), said: 'This survey confirms the huge pressure on young people to fit in with their friends and peer groups. It is incredibly sad to hear how many youngsters are bullied or isolated for not having the same clothes or accessories as their classmates. Advertising and marketing have made our society increasingly image-conscious and our children are suffering the consequences.

'Schools and colleges should be places where all children feel equal, but it is virtually impossible for schools to protect their pupils from the harsher aspects of these commercial influences.

'We are worried these pressures will further intensify as schools and colleges look for more help from commercial sponsors to provide IT, sports and science equipment, teaching materials and food.'

11 August 2008

⇨ The above information is reprinted with kind permission from ATL, the education union. Visit www.atl.org.uk for more information.

© *ATL*

Online bullying

Information from Becta

Children and young people are keen adopters of new technologies, but this can also leave them open to the threat of increased bullying – known as online bullying, e-bullying or cyberbullying. Online bullying can be defined as follows:

'The use of information and communication technologies such as email, [mobile] phone and text messages, instant messaging, defamatory personal websites and defamatory personal polling websites, to support deliberate, repeated, and hostile behaviour by an individual or a group, that is intended to harm others.'
[Bill Belsey, www.cyberbullying.ca]

An awareness of the issues and knowledge of methods for dealing with online bullying can help reduce the risks.

Bullying by text message

Bullying by text message has become an unfortunate and unpleasant by-product of the convenience that SMS (short message service) offers. Texting is more casual than a phone call and messages can be sent and received at times when other communication is not convenient. It is also perceived as being more anonymous, particularly if the message is sent via a website. Sometimes text messages are sent to embarrass, threaten or bully someone. This can be particularly upsetting as the message can arrive when the receiver least expects it. Additionally, if the person's number is not listed in the receiver's address book then the receiver will not necessarily know who has sent the message.

Children should be advised to be careful about giving out their mobile phone number, and ask that those that have their number never pass it on – if only known and trusted friends know the number, the less likely it is to be abused in this way.

If being bullied by text message, children should immediately seek help from a teacher, parent or carer. They should not respond to the messages, but should keep a detailed diary recording information such as the content of the message, the date, the time, the caller ID or whether the number was withheld or not available. The messages should also be stored on the phone in case they are needed later as evidence. Abuse in the form of bullying should be reported to the mobile phone company who can take certain steps to try to resolve the situation, and in some instances it may also be necessary to involve the police.

In some cases it may be necessary, or easier, to change the mobile phone number or to purchase a new phone.

Bullying by email

Like bullying by text message, email provides a reasonably 'anonymous' method of communication which bullies have seized upon to harass their victims.

If being bullied by email, children should not respond to the messages, but should seek help from a teacher, parent or carer. Likewise if they receive an email message from an unknown sender, they should exercise caution over opening it, or ask an adult for assistance. Don't delete the message but keep it as evidence of bullying.

If the email is being sent from a personal email account, abuse should be reported to the sender's email service provider. Many email programs also provide facilities to block email from certain senders.

If the bullying emails continue, and the email address of the sender is not obvious, then it may be possible to track the address using special software. Your email service provider may be able to offer assistance in doing this.

In certain cases, it may be easier to change your email address, and exercise caution over who this new address is given to.

Bullying within chat rooms or by instant messaging

Aside from the general risks of using chat rooms and instant messaging (IM) services, these services are also used by bullies.

Chat is a way of communicating with numerous people at the same time by typing messages which immediately appear on screen in a virtual meeting place, known as a chat room. Chat rooms have an element of anonymity so children may often have the confidence to say things online which they would not say face to face. While this can be a positive thing for some children, it can also lead to bullying. Groups are often formed in chat rooms, just as they would be in school, and can be used as a way of excluding or harassing others.

Children should be encouraged to always use moderated chat rooms, and to never give out personal information while chatting. If bullying does occur, they should not respond to messages, but should leave the chat room, and seek advice from a teacher, parent or carer. If using a moderated chat room,

the system moderators should also be informed, giving as much detail as possible, so that they can take appropriate action.

IM is a form of online chat but is private between two or more people. The system works on the basis of 'buddy lists', where chat can only take place with those on your list. Children should only add people to their buddy list that they know, and reject requests from others to join their list. Although this effectively reduces the risk of being bullied by IM, abuse is still possible.

If a child is bullied or harassed by IM, the service provider should be informed giving the nickname or ID, date, time and details of the problem. The service provider will then take appropriate action which could involve a warning or disconnection from the IM service. If a child has experienced bullying in this way, it might also be worth re-registering for instant messaging with a new user ID.

Bullying by websites

Bullying via websites is also an issue. Such bullying generally takes the form of websites that mock, torment, harass or are otherwise offensive, often aimed at an individual or group of people.

If a child discovers a bullying website referring to them, they should immediately seek help from a teacher, parent or carer. Pages should be copied and printed from the website concerned for evidence, and the Internet service provider (ISP) responsible for hosting the site should be contacted immediately. The ISP can take steps to find out who posted the site, and request that it is removed. Many ISPs will outline their procedures for dealing with reported abuse in an acceptable use policy (AUP) which can be found on their website.

Additionally, many websites and forum services now provide facilities for visitors to create online votes and polls, which have been used by bullies to humiliate and embarrass their fellow pupils. Again, any misuse of such services should be reported to a teacher, parent or carer who should then take steps to contact the hosting website and request the removal of the poll.

Last modified 16 May 2008

⇨ The above information is re-printed with kind permission from Becta. Visit www.becta.org.uk for more information.

© Becta

Cyberbullying

A whole-school community issue

Cyberbullying, A *whole-school community issue* is a summary of the Department for Children, Schools and Families (DCSF) Guidance for schools on preventing and responding to cyberbullying, which was written in conjunction with Childnet International and published in September 2007. This document seeks to give practical advice to young people, their carers and school staff about the issue of cyberbullying.

Introduction

Today's children and young people have grown up in a world that is very different from that of most adults. Many young people experience the Internet and mobile phones as a

positive, productive and creative part of their activities and development of their identities; always on and always there. Above all, information communication technologies support social activity that allows young people to feel connected to their peers.

Unfortunately, technologies are also being used negatively. When children are the target of bullying via mobiles phones or the Internet, they can feel alone and very misunderstood. They may not be able to identify that what is happening to them is a form of bullying, or be confident that the adults around them will understand it that way either. Previously safe and enjoyable environments and activities can become threatening and a source

of anxiety.

As mobile phone and Internet use become increasingly common, so has the misuse of this technology to bully. Current research in this area indicates that cyberbullying is a feature of many young people's lives. One study carried out for the Anti-Bullying Alliance found that 22% of young people reported being the target of cyberbullying.

This document explains how cyberbullying is different from other forms of bullying, how to respond and combat misuse through a shared responsibility, and how to promote and develop a culture of confident technology users to support innovation, e-safety and digital literacy skills.

What is cyberbullying?

Cyberbullying is the use of Information Communications Technology (ICT), particularly mobile phones and the Internet, deliberately to upset someone else.

What's different about cyberbullying?

Bullying is not new, but some features of cyberbullying are different from other forms of bullying:

1 24/7 and the invasion of home/personal space. Cyberbullying can take place at any time and can intrude into spaces that have previously been regarded as safe or personal.

2 The audience can be very large and reached rapidly. The difficulty in controlling electronically circulated messages means the scale and scope of cyberbullying can be greater than for other forms of bullying. Electronically forwarded content is hard to control, and the worry of content resurfacing can make it difficult for targets to move on.

3 People who cyberbully may attempt to remain anonymous. This can be extremely distressing for those being bullied. The person cyberbullying may never be in the same physical space as their target.

4 The profile of the bully and target. Cyberbullying can take place both between peers and across generations; teachers have also been targets. Age or size are not important. Bystanders can also become accessories to the bullying; for example, by passing on a humiliating image.

5 Some instances of cyberbullying are known to be unintentional. It can be the result of not thinking (something sent as a joke may be deeply upsetting or offensive to the recipient) or a lack of awareness of the consequences – for example saying something negative online about another pupil, or friend that they don't expect to be forwarded or viewed outside their immediate group.

6 Many cyberbullying incidents can themselves act as evidence. This is one of the reasons why it's important to know how to respond!

Cyberbullying and the law

Education law: Bullying is never acceptable. The school community has a duty to protect all its members and provide a safe, healthy environment. A range of Education Acts and government initiatives highlight these obligations.

The Education and Inspections Act 2006 (EIA 2006) outlines some legal powers which relate more directly to cyberbullying. Head teachers have the power 'to such an extent as is reasonable' to regulate the conduct of pupils when they are off site. The EIA also provides a defence for school staff in confiscating items such as mobile phones from pupils.

Civil and criminal law: Although bullying is not a specific criminal offence in UK law, there are laws that can apply in terms of harassing or threatening behaviour, for example, or indeed menacing and threatening communications. In fact, some cyberbullying activities could be criminal offences under a range of different laws, including the Protection from Harassment Act 1997, which has both criminal and civil provision, the Malicious Communications Act 1988, section 127 of the Communications Act 2003, and the Public Order Act 1986.

'I felt that no one understood what I was going through. I didn't know who was sending me these messages, and I felt powerless to know what to do.'

A pupil

Preventing cyberbullying

The best way to deal with cyberbullying is to prevent it happening in the first place. The key first step is deciding who within the school community will take responsibility for the coordination and implementation of cyberbullying prevention and response strategies. It's best if this person is a member of the school's senior management team and/or the staff member responsible for coordinating overall anti-bullying activity. This person will need to have experience of making sure the whole school community contribute to, and are included in, activities.

There is no single solution to the problem of cyberbullying. These are the five key areas schools need to address together to put in place a comprehensive and effective prevention plan:

1. Understanding and talking about cyberbullying

The whole school community needs a shared, agreed definition of cyberbullying. Everyone needs to be aware of the impact of cyberbullying and the ways in which it differs from other forms of bullying. Young people and their parents should be made aware of pupils' responsibilities in their use of ICT, and what the sanctions are for misuse. Students and parents should know that the school can provide them with support if cyberbullying takes place out of school.

2. Updating existing policies and practices

Review and update the school's anti-bullying policy plus other relevant policies – for example, policies on behaviour, pastoral care and e-learning strategies. Review your existing Acceptable Use Policies (AUPs) – the rules that students have to agree to follow in order to use ICT in school – and publicise them to parents and students. Keep good records of any incidents of cyberbullying. Be able to conduct searches of Internet use records at school. Knowing that the school is taking such steps may act as a disincentive for bullies to misuse school equipment and systems.

3. Making reporting cyberbullying easier

No one should feel that they have to deal with cyberbullying alone, but reporting any incident of bullying can be really hard for the person being bullied and for bystanders. Provide and publicise different ways of reporting cyberbullying in schools – for instance, a student council taskforce, peer reporting, anonymous reporting – and provide information about contacting service providers directly.

4. Promoting the positive use of technology

Technology is successfully being used to support engaging, positive and effective learning, and to realise and increase the potential of personalised learning by making learning more flexible, creative and accessible. Explore safe ways of using technology with learners to support self-esteem, assertiveness, participation and to develop friendships. Promote and discuss 'netiquette', e-safety and digital literacy. Show learners that the adults in the school understand the technologies they use – or get the students to teach them!

5. Evaluating the impact of prevention activities

Regular reviews are vital to make sure that antibullying policies are working and are up to date. Consider conducting an annual survey of pupils' experiences of bullying, including cyberbullying, and a parent satisfaction survey. Publicise progress and activities to the whole-school community – keep cyberbullying a live issue and celebrate your successes!

'Having my daughter show me text messages from nearly everyone in her class, all saying derogatory things about her, was devastating.'
A parent

Responding to cyberbullying

Cyberbullying is a form of bullying, and therefore all schools should already be equipped to deal with the majority of cases through their existing anti-bullying policies and procedures. This section outlines key steps to take when responding to cyberbullying.

Supporting the person being bullied

⇨ Give reassurance that the person has done the right thing by telling someone, refer to any existing pastoral support/procedures and inform parents.
⇨ Advise on next steps:
  ↳ Make sure the person knows not to retaliate or return the message.
  ↳ Ask the person to think about

what information they have in the public domain.
  ↳ Help the person to keep relevant evidence for any investigation (e.g. by not deleting messages they've received, and by taking screen capture shots and noting web addresses of online cyber-bullying instances).
  ↳ Check the person understands simple ways to prevent it from happening again, e.g. by changing contact details, blocking contacts or leaving a chatroom.
⇨ Take action to contain the in-cident when content has been circulated:
  ↳ If you know who the person responsible is, ask them to remove the content.
  ↳ Contact the host (e.g. the social networking site) to make a report to get the content taken down.
  ↳ Use disciplinary powers to confiscate phones that are being used to cyberbully. Ask the pupil to tell you who they have sent messages on to.
  ↳ In cases of illegal content, contact the police, who can determine what needs to be kept for evidential purposes.

Investigating incidents

All bullying incidents should be properly recorded and investigated. Cyberbullying can be a very serious matter and can constitute a criminal offence. In UK law, there are criminal laws that can apply in terms of harassment or threatening and menacing communications.

⇨ Advise pupils and staff to try and keep a record of the bullying as evidence. It can be useful to show parents, teachers, pastoral care staff and the police, if necessary, what has happened.
⇨ Take steps to identify the bul-ly, including looking at the school systems, identifying and interviewing possible witnesses, and contacting the service provider and the police, if necessary. The police will need to be involved to enable the service provider to look into the data of another user.

Working with the bully and

sanctions

Once the person bullying is identified, steps should be taken to change their attitude and behaviour as well as ensuring access to any support that is required. Factors to consider when determining the appropriate sanctions include:

⇨ The impact on the victim: was the bully acting anonymously, was the material widely circulated and humiliating, how difficult was controlling the spread of the material?
⇨ The motivation of the bully: was the incident unintentional or retaliation to bullying behaviour from others?

Technology-specific sanctions for pupils engaged in cyberbullying behaviour could include limiting Internet access for a period of time or removing the right to bring a mobile into school.

'Thankfully, my son's school was very helpful: they identified the child who posted the video from another video he had posted; they have disciplined the other child and had him remove the video.'
A parent

Key safety advice

The whole school community has a part to play in ensuring cyber safety. Understanding children and young people's online lives and activities can help adults respond to situations appropriately and effectively. Asking children and young people to show adults how technologies and services work is a useful strategy that can provide an important learning opportunity and context for discus-sing online safety.

For children and young people

1 Always respect others – be careful what you say online and what images you send.
2 Think before you send – whatever you send can be made public very quickly and could stay online for ever.
3 Treat your password like your toothbrush – keep it to yourself. Only give your mobile number or personal website address to trusted friends.
4 Block the bully – learn how to block or report someone who is

behaving badly.

5 Don't retaliate or reply!

6 Save the evidence – learn how to keep records of offending messages, pictures or online conversations.

7 Make sure you tell:
- ↳ an adult you trust, or call a helpline like ChildLine on 0800 1111 in confidence;
- ↳ the provider of the service; check the service provider's website to see where to report incidents;
- ↳ your school – your teacher or the anti-bullying coordinator can help you.

Finally, don't just stand there – if you see cyberbullying going on, support the victim and report the bullying. How would you feel if no one stood up for you?

For parents and carers

1 Be aware, your child may as likely cyberbully as be a target of cyberbullying. Be alert to your child seeming upset after using the Internet or their mobile phone. This might involve subtle comments or changes in relationships with friends. They might be unwilling to talk or be secretive about their online activities and mobile phone use.

2 Talk with your children and understand the ways in which they are using the Internet and their mobile phone. See the seven key messages for children (on the left) to get you started.

3 Use the tools on the service and turn on in-built Internet safety features.

4 Remind your child not to retaliate.

5 Keep the evidence of offending emails, text messages or online conversations.

6 Report cyberbullying:
- ↳ Contact your child's school if it involves another pupil, so that they can take appropriate action.
- ↳ Contact the service provider.
- ↳ If the cyberbullying is serious and a potential criminal offence has been committed, you should consider contacting the police.

September 2007

⇨ The above information is reprinted with kind permission from the Department for Children, Schools and Families. Visit www.dcsf.gov.uk for more information on this and other topics.

© Crown copyright

Technology: use and misuse

Technology can be used both positively and negatively. The table below explores the range of ways today's technology can be used.

Technology	Great for:	Examples of misuse
Mobile phones	Keeping in touch by voice or text, taking and sending pictures and film, listening to music, playing games, going online and sending emails. Useful in emergency situations and for allowing children a greater sense of independence.	Sending nasty calls or text messages, including threats, intimidation, harassment. Taking and sharing humiliating images. Videoing other people being harassed and sending these to other phones or Internet sites.
Instant Messenger (IM)	Text or voice chatting live with friends online. A quick and effective way of keeping in touch even while working on other things.	Sending nasty messages or content. Using someone else's account to forward rude or mean messages via their contacts list.
Chatrooms and message boards	Groups of people around the world can text or voice chat live about common interests. For young people, this can be an easy way to meet new people and explore issues which they are too shy to talk about in person.	Sending nasty or threatening anonymous messages. Groups of people deciding to pick on or ignore individuals. Making friends under false pretences – people pretending to be someone they're not in order to get personal information that they can misuse in a range of ways – e.g. by spreading secrets or blackmailing.
Email	Sending electronic letters, pictures and other files quickly and cheaply anywhere in the world.	Sending nasty or threatening messages. Forwarding unsuitable content including images and video clips, or sending computer viruses. Accessing someone else's account, e.g. to forward personal emails or delete emails.
Webcams	Taking pictures or recording messages. Being able to see and talk to someone live on your computer screen. Bringing far-off places to life or video conferencing.	Making and sending inappropriate content. Persuading or threatening young people to act in inappropriate ways. Using inappropriate recordings to manipulate young people.
Social network sites	Socialising with your friends and making new ones within online communities. Allowing young people to be creative online, even publishing online music. Personalising homepages and profiles, creating and uploading content.	Posting nasty comments, humiliating images/video. Accessing another person's account details and sending unpleasant messages, deleting information or making private information public. Groups of people picking on individuals by excluding them. Creating fake profiles to pretend to be someone else, e.g. to bully, harass or get the person into trouble.
Video hosting sites	Accessing useful educational, entertaining and original creative video content and uploading your own.	Posting embarrassing, humiliating film of someone.
Virtual Learning Environments (VLEs)	School site, usually available from home and school, set up for tracking and recording student assignments, tests and activities, with message boards, chat and IM.	Posting inappropriate messages or images. Hacking into someone else's account to post inappropriate comments or delete schoolwork.
Gaming sites, consoles and virtual worlds	Live text or voice chat during online gaming between players across the world, or on handheld consoles with people in the same local area. Virtual worlds let users design their own avatars – a figure that represents them in the virtual world.	Name-calling, making abusive/derogatory remarks. Players may pick on weaker or less experienced users, repeatedly killing their characters. Forwarding unwanted messages to other devices in the immediate vicinity.

Source: 'Scrabbling: a whole-school community issue', Department for Children, Schools and Families, September 2007. Crown copyright.

A million online bullies run rampant in cyberspace

Information from Garlik

Britain's playground bullies are increasingly moving online to harass and abuse their victims.

A new study published by online identity experts Garlik charts the number of young net bullies in the UK. One in five 8- to 15-year-olds (18 per cent) freely admit to being online bullies and posting deliberately offensive comments about others and in extreme cases 'stealing' their identities.

The motivation for this bad behaviour varies with the majority of culprits (30 per cent) admitting they do it because it's fun, one in seven (13 per cent) say it's the only place they can act like this without getting into trouble and one in twenty because it makes them feel powerful. In addition, one in twelve (8 per cent) are pressured into this online misdemeanour by their friends.

And whilst the majority of parents (61 per cent) are in the dark about their offspring's bad behaviour, a quarter of the young online bullies state their parents know about their actions and think it's harmless fun.

The Garlik research, which questioned 1,000 8- to 15-year-olds and parents across the UK, also reveals the impact of this cyber misconduct. At least 2.3 million online incidents have taken place, affecting four in ten (43 per cent) young people in the UK.

One in six (15 per cent) have been cyber-bullied – a 4 per cent increase on last year – close to one in ten (9 per cent) have been ridiculed on their social networking site and a similar number (8 per cent) have had their identity 'stolen' for malicious use or intent.

One in five 8- to 15-year-olds (18 per cent) freely admit to being online bullies and posting deliberately offensive comments about others and in extreme cases 'stealing' their identities

---

The online identity experts warn that cyber misconduct is vastly underestimated as the majority of incidents go unreported – 60 per cent of victims fail to tell their parents.

Tom Ilube, CEO of Garlik, said: 'Our research demonstrates cyber misconduct is real and growing, with bullies using the web as an additional weapon in their armoury. What does it say about the way our society is changing that such a high number of young people use the Internet's veil of anonymity to bully and abuse their peers?'

Ilube continues: 'Bullying is a frequent occurrence in the playground, but now as bullies move online there is increasingly no escape. Parents need to closely track their children's online activities to ensure they are acting responsibly online.'

John Carr, an expert on child safety on the Internet, said: 'New technologies always seem to bring with them a series of unintended and unforeseen consequences. In the case of the Internet and mobile phones bullying is definitely one of them. Bullying can ruin children's lives. As the long school holidays approach, this research is a timely reminder of the importance of parents and teachers engaging with children, to remind them of how serious the consequences of bullying can be, both for the victim and the perpetrator, but also to encourage them to speak out if it happens to them or any of their friends.'
3 July 2008

⇨ The above information is reprinted with kind permission from Garlik. Visit www.garlik.com for more information.

© *Garlik*

Prevalence of cyberbullying

Over 60% of secondary teachers say pupils have been affected by cyberbullying, according to an ATL survey

With the increase of electronic intimidation 64% of secondary school teachers say pupils have been victims of cyberbullying, according to a survey carried out by the Association of Teachers and Lecturers (ATL).

In addition 16% of teachers have themselves been victims of cyberbullying and of those more than half have received silent calls or been the victims of videoing, which has been posted on websites such as YouTube.

The survey found that pupils are mostly being bullied by text with 70% of secondary teachers believing that where cyberbullying takes place, pupils have received unwelcome messages. Among junior pupils teachers say 60% of cyberbullying takes the form of threatening messages via an Internet chat room.

Margaret Upton, a teacher from the North East, said: 'The school is making every effort to keep students off web sites such as BEBO but this is proving difficult. Students go on these sites at home and the upset from some of the messages then affects school.'

Matt Whittaker from Burleigh College, Leicestershire, added: 'An area I am very aware of, due to it affecting my own children, is pornography on phones and the ease of file sharing. My 11-year-old girl watches hardcore porn in school playgrounds and I can't do anything about it. This is child abuse. Parents need to be made aware of what their kid's video with Bluetooth phones are being used for because it's not for talking to each other on.'

A survey of over 250 teachers working in state schools throughout the UK in February found that 67% of junior school teachers have themselves received unwelcome emails and text messages, and almost 40% of secondary teachers have been the victims of videoing.

Further distinctions were found in the results from junior and secondary school teachers when 68% of secondary teachers believed that the perpetrator of this cyberbullying was a pupil while none of the junior school teachers knew who the perpetrator was.

ATL general secretary, Dr Mary Bousted, said: 'Cyberbullying, as with all forms of bullying, is totally unacceptable and no teacher or pupil should have to endure it. With the majority of this bullying taking place outside school, it is difficult to police. Schools should ensure that they have a rigorous Code of Conduct to address cyberbullying, which all staff and pupils are aware of and perpetrators of such bullying should be held to account for their actions.'

Tami Buckingham from St Andrew's RC School, Surrey, said: 'Due to the extensive use of mobiles the vast majority of cases go unreported. Many teachers are embarrassed or blissfully (and deliberately) unaware of comments on sites such as ratemyteacher. Punishment for pupils especially when starting or spreading rumours about staff is not stiff enough to act as a deterrent.'

Peter Richardson from Enniskillen Collegiate, Northern Ireland, said: 'Cyberbullying is very difficult to police as online users can retain anonymity quite easily. For a school this is a major issue. Most of the responses to cyberbullying are reactive rather than proactive so the damage to pupil or teacher has been done.'

John Ross from Hemel Hempstead School, Hertfordshire, said: 'Some of this is perpetrated outside school where we have little control. The school systems have a county-based blocking system but pupils who have the expertise can find ways of by-passing these security measures.'

Junior school teachers also said cyberbullying reduced their confidence and self-esteem, made them ill or stressed, and made them scared outside work.

Penny Black from Taverham High School in Norfolk said: 'I believe that it must be acted upon quickly and effectively. It is not enough to say that as it did not happen in school perhaps, that it is not "our problem". I think it is a problem we need to deal with in school if the children doing it attend the school.'

18 March 2008

⇨ The above information is reprinted with kind permission from ATL, the education union. Visit www.atl.org.uk for more information.

© ATL

Keeping cyberspace safe

Government launches new UK council for child Internet safety

Some of the biggest names from industry and charities have joined forces with the Government, parents and young people to help keep children safe online, Children's Secretary Ed Balls and Home Secretary Jacqui Smith announced today.

The new UK Council for Child Internet Safety (UKCCIS) will unite over 100 organisations from the public and private sector working with Government to deliver recommendations from Dr Tanya Byron's report 'Safer Children in a Digital World'.

Reporting directly to the Prime Minister, the Council will help to improve the regulation and education around Internet use, tackling problems around online bullying, safer search features, and violent video games. This unprecedented coalition of experts and organisations will ensure that parents and young people have a voice in the development of a Child Internet Safety Strategy, to be delivered early next year.

The strategy will:

⇨ establish a comprehensive public information and awareness and child Internet safety campaign across Government and industry including a 'one-stop shop' on child Internet safety;

⇨ provide specific measures to support vulnerable children and young people, such as taking down illegal Internet sites that promote harmful behaviour;

⇨ promote responsible advertising to children online; and

⇨ establish voluntary codes of practice for user-generated content sites, making such sites commit to take down inappropriate content within a given time.

Speaking at the launch of the UKCCIS at the Science Museum in London, Children's Minister Ed Balls said:

'Today's launch is a significant achievement and I thank all members of the Council for their support and commitment. We want to help children and young people to make the most of what all digital and interactive technologies can offer. By putting in place the right support for children, young people and parents we can reduce much of the anxiety that exists around the Internet. UKCISS will enable everyone from parents to industry, Government, education, and children's welfare organisations to play their part in keeping children safe online.'

The Council will help to improve the regulation and education around Internet use, tackling problems around online bullying, safer search features, and violent video games

---

Home Secretary Jacqui Smith said:

'We are determined to do all we can to ensure that the Internet environment is safe for children to use. Earlier this year, the Home Office published the first ever social networking guidance developed with industry, charities and law enforcement.

'The new UK Council builds on this by bringing together over one hundred organisations all committed to keeping children safe online. By working in partnership we can intensify our efforts to protect young people.'

Review author Dr Tanya Byron said:

'Every parent will know that video games and the Internet are a part of childhood like never before. This is extremely positive; giving kids the opportunities to learn to have fun and communicate in ways that previous generations could only dream of. But it can also present a huge challenge to parents and other adults involved in the welfare of children.

'That is why we need industry, regulators and parents to work together to protect children against the risks. Setting up UKCISS was a key recommendation in my report and I'm delighted that the Government along with industry, education, law enforcement, and the children's charities have acted so promptly to make this a reality.

'The Council will be a powerful union of some of our key players giving

and as a company, we are working hard to ensure that the Internet is as safe an environment as possible. All of us who are concerned for the welfare of children, or have children of our own, welcome the formation of this council and its objective of protecting young people in the digital world.'

The Government also announced today the successful appointees to the Council's Executive Board. Chaired by DCSF and HO Ministers, the Board includes senior representation from across Government, industry, the third sector, law enforcement and the devolved administrations. UKCCIS will report annually to the Prime Minister at the Child Internet Safety Summit.

29 September 2008

⇨ The above information is reprinted with kind permission from the Department for Children, Schools and Families. Visit www.dcsf.gov.uk for more information.

© *Crown copyright*

support to parents and guidance to children as they come more and more accustomed to the virtual world – it will also give families, teachers and most importantly children and young people the ability to input experiences and concerns. The UK is a world leader on Internet safety for children and I look forward to others adopting this partnership approach.'

Culture Secretary Andy Burnham said:

'We all know the number of benefits the Internet has brought to our day-to-day lives. But it has also raised questions about how we can and should protect the public, and particularly children, in this online space. To our very great benefit, we've embraced the online world wholeheartedly, but we must ensure that what is unacceptable offline should not be acceptable online. The UK Council for Child Internet Safety will allow all stakeholders to work together in finding appropriate ways of maintaining the standards of the online material that young people have access to.'

Matthew Bishop at Microsoft said:

'The Internet opens a door into all our homes. It is perhaps the single greatest innovation for expanding the horizons of knowledge and creativity. But, as with all human growth and exploration these benefits come hand in hand with elements of risk, especially for children. As an industry,

Happy slapping

Information from BullyingUK

Happy slapping is the wrong description for an assault in which the attack is filmed. There's nothing happy about it, it's a bit like calling someone who steals a car and kills someone a 'joyrider'.

Bullying UK started to get complaints about happy slapping in November 2004. The first incidents took place in the London area, often on buses and trains, and quickly spread to the school playground and street.

What is happy slapping?

The assault usually involves a stranger being hit over the head while other members of the gang take photographs/video on their camera phones. The pictures are then circulated by mobile phone or put on the Internet. In recent months happy slapping has become an unpleasant and dangerous craze. There have been a number of high profile cases in which attackers have been jailed for killing people in this way.

Where happy slapping attacks have happened in school playgrounds pupils have been afraid to return to school. Anyone who thinks this is just a bit of harmless fun should think about the consequences.

Anyone assaulted in this way should tell their parents who should make a complaint to the police.

Happy slapping is a criminal offence

There are a number of offences involved. The first is assault, the second is harassment if the pictures are shown around and uploaded to the Internet and it may also be against telecommunications law.

Bullying UK has had numerous complaints about abusive videos uploaded to websites like YouTube. If you or your friends are the victim of a filmed assault let us know on help@bullying.co.uk and we'll advise you how to get the material removed.

Some schools have already banned mobile phones from being used during the day to prevent pupils sending abusive text messages. We're now hearing of others banning them after happy slapping incidents. It's unfortunate that the bad behaviour of a tiny minority of pupils inconveniences everyone but if head teachers think there is a risk of assaults on the premises then they need to protect pupils and a ban on phones on the premises is probably the best way to do that.

⇨ The above information is reprinted with kind permission from BullyingUK. Visit www.bullying.co.uk for more information.

© *BullyingUK*

Bullying in the workplace

You shouldn't have to put up with bullying at work. Read about what bullying is and how to tell if you're being bullied, and details of what you can do to stop it

What is bullying at work?

Bullying at work is when someone tries to intimidate another worker, often in front of colleagues. It's usually, though not always, done to someone in a less senior position.

It's similar to harassment, which is where someone's behaviour is offensive – for example, making sexual comments, or abusing someone's race, religion or sexual orientation.

It's not possible to make a legal claim directly about bullying, but complaints can be made under laws covering discrimination and harassment. If you're forced to resign due to bullying you can make a constructive dismissal claim.

Examples of bullying behaviour

Bullying includes abuse, physical or verbal violence, humiliation and undermining someone's confidence. You are probably being bullied if, for example, you're:

⇨ constantly picked on;
⇨ humiliated in front of colleagues;
⇨ regularly unfairly treated;
⇨ physically or verbally abused;
⇨ blamed for problems caused by others;
⇨ always given too much to do, so that you regularly fail in your work;
⇨ regularly threatened with the sack;
⇨ unfairly passed over for promotion or denied training opportunities.

Bullying can be face to face, in writing, over the phone or by fax or email.

Before taking action

If you think you're being bullied, it's best to talk it over with someone, because what seems like bullying might not be. For example, you might have more work to do because of a change in the way your organisation is run. If you find it difficult to cope, talk to your manager or supervisor, who might be as concerned as you are. Sometimes all it takes is a change in the way you work to give you time to adjust.

What to do if you're bullied at work

Employers have a 'duty of care' to their employees and this includes dealing with bullying at work. There are measures you can take if you're being bullied.

Get advice

Speak to someone about how you might deal with the problem informally. This might be:

⇨ an employee representative like a trade union official;
⇨ someone in the firm's human resources department;
⇨ your manager or supervisor.

Some employers have specially trained staff to help with bullying and harassment problems. They're sometimes called 'harassment advisers'. If the bullying is affecting your health, visit your GP.

Talk to the bully

The bullying may not be deliberate. If you can, talk to the person in question, who may not realise how their behaviour has been affecting you. Work out what to say beforehand. Describe what's been happening and why you object to it. Stay calm and be polite. If you don't want to talk to them yourself, ask someone else to do so for you.

Keep a written record or diary

Write down details of every incident and keep copies of any relevant documents.

Make a formal complaint

This is the next step if you can't solve the problem informally. To do this you must follow your employer's grievance procedure, or if one doesn't exist you can use the statutory grievance procedure.

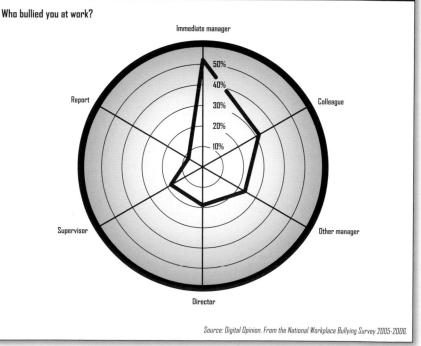

Who bullied you at work?

Who bullied you at work?

Immediate manager
Colleague
Other manager
Director
Supervisor
Report

50%
40%
30%
20%
10%

Source: Digital Opinion. From the National Workplace Bullying Survey 2005-2006.

Some awkward situations

The bully is your manager, but the firm's grievance procedure says that's who you should speak to

Make the complaint in writing to your line manager, and ask that it's passed on to another manager to look into. If that doesn't happen or isn't possible, make the complaint to your boss's manager, or the human resources department.

The person bullying you is a sole trader or the firm's managing director or owner

Follow the grievance procedure. It may help you later if you have to take legal action against your employer.

Your boss is violent and abusive towards you and you're afraid to make a complaint

If you think that making a complaint will cause further bullying or harassment, you don't need to follow normal grievance procedures. In cases like this, you can still then take legal action if you wish.

What about taking legal action?

Sometimes the problem continues even after you've followed your employer's grievance procedure. If nothing is done to put things right, you can think about legal action, which may mean going to an employment tribunal. Get professional advice before taking this step.

Remember that it's not possible to go to a tribunal directly over bullying, but complaints can be made under laws covering discrimination and harassment.

If you've left your job because of bullying, you might be able to claim unfair 'constructive' dismissal. This can be difficult to prove, so it's important to get advice from a specialist lawyer or other professional.

⇨ The above information is reprinted with kind permission from Directgov. Visit www.direct.gov.uk for more information.

© Crown copyright

Three and a half million bullied in job

Information from the Trades Union Congress

Three and a half million people (14 per cent or one in seven of the workforce) say they have been bullied in their current job according to a YouGov poll for the TUC published today (Friday). 21 per cent (one in five) say that bullying is an issue where they work.

Bullying is more likely in the public sector where 19 per cent say they have been bullied compared to 12 per cent in the private sector and eight per cent in the voluntary sector.

Surprisingly people in professional and associate professional jobs are the most likely to be bullied (16 per cent). This may reflect the large number of professional and associate professional jobs in the public sector such as teaching, and across the NHS.

Men are more likely to be bullied (16 per cent) than women (12 per cent). 45- to 54-year-olds (19 per cent), followed by 35- to 44-year-olds (17 per cent) are the age groups most likely to be bullied. 25- to 34-year-olds are the least bullied (8 per cent).

The East Midlands workforce is the most bullied at 18 per cent, with the East of England the least (eight per cent).

Bullying is more likely in the public sector where 19 per cent say they have been bullied compared to 12 per cent in the private sector and eight per cent in the voluntary sector

---

It is not the low paid who are most likely to say they are bullied. Those earning less than £20,000 report much less bullying than those earning between £20,000 and £60,000 (17 per cent). But among those earning above £60,000 only seven per cent say they are bullied.

TUC General Secretary Brendan Barber said: 'This level of bullying at work is completely unacceptable. It is particularly disturbing that more people complain of bullying in the public sector. Every organisation needs to have an anti-bullying policy, and every manager should ensure that there is zero-tolerance of bullying either by line managers or workmates.'

Recognition and awareness of workplace bullying is essential if it is to be legitimately challenged. The TUC fully supports and endorses the work of the Andrea Adams Trust, who run a national annual campaign to raise awareness of the issue, culminating in Ban Bullying at Work Day held on 7 November.

Andrea Adams Trust Chief Executive Lyn Witheridge said: 'We encourage every employer to become involved and use this opportunity to participate in the wide array of activities provided by the Ban Bullying at Work Day campaign.'

5 September 2008

⇨ The above information is reprinted with kind permission from the Trades Union Congress. Visit www.tuc.org.uk for more information.

© Trades Union Congress

Workplace bullying rife

Rising stress levels hit the health of the nation and the economy

Bullying in the UK is endemic and for one in four people it is a weekly or even daily cause of stress. Over 80% of workers have been bullied during their careers and a third of people are so stressed they have dreamed of quitting for a life abroad. Over half say their jobs are getting more stressful and that work is overtaking their home lives.

These are the key findings of Samaritans' survey for Stress Down Day, which took place on Friday 1 February 2008. Stress Down Day is a national campaign to encourage people to take better care of their health at work and reduce currently damaging stress levels: visit www.stressdownday.org to find out more.

Bullying in the UK is endemic and for one in four people it is a weekly or even daily cause of stress

---

Samaritans' Joe Ferns said: 'Job-related stress has a serious and unrecognised impact on the health of the nation and the economy, affecting concentration and efficiency. Thirteen million working days were lost to stress, depression and anxiety in 2005 at a staggering cost of 3.7 billion to UK plc.

'Positive workplaces are a big factor in keeping everyone emotionally healthy. There is not enough openness and that is what Stress Down Day is all about; encouraging employers and employees to speak out and discuss problems before they escalate.'

Young employees (18-24 years) are most vulnerable to stress, with 38% feeling less likely than all other age groups to talk openly to their managers and 57% unable to talk to colleagues. Forty-eight per cent are more likely to be bullied by clients and customers whereas over half of other age groups reported being bullied by their managers.

Occupation has a major influence on stress, with over 40% of IT workers, retailers, caterers and engineers feeling unsupported at work and over half unable to deal with stress, compared with people in health, education, banking and finance over half of whom claim they receive adequate support at work.

Samaritans Stressed Out survey also shows that:
⇨ 49% of people are worried about the effect stress is having on their health, compared with 44% of people last year.
⇨ 32% of workers feel their employers turn a blind eye to the problem of stress and 43% feel their bosses try to get as much out of them as possible, regardless of their stress levels.
⇨ Over half have seen colleagues cry over pressure and 83% would rather say they were sick with flu or another problem rather than admit they were stressed.
⇨ There is still a large gender imbalance when it comes to sharing domestic stress; with three-quarters of women in the UK taking sole responsibility for domestic tasks.

Professor Cary Cooper of Lancaster University, an internationally recognised expert in the field of workplace stress, said: 'These results really disturb me. Shouldn't we be managing people by reward and praise rather than by fault finding and bullying?

'We know that dealing with difficult people issues can be lonely and frustrating. The message from Samaritans is that you are not alone. Employees need more support from work colleagues and line managers and everyone needs coping skills to help them deal with everyday pressures.'

Samaritans runs WorkLife, a training course to tackle stress in the workplace and provide practical skills for managers and team members. Log on to www.stressdownday.org for more information. A CD-ROM of the course is also available.

Samaritans surveyed 2,100 adults in the UK and 500 adults in the Republic of Ireland, through nfpSynergy between 12 and 30 November 2007.
16 January 2008

Note
Stress Down Day 2009 will be taking place on Friday 6 February.

⇨ The above information is re-printed with kind permission from Samaritans. Visit www.samaritans.org for more information.

© *Samaritans*

The hidden menace: bullying at work

Information from HR Zone

Sticks and stones may break my bones but words can also hurt me. Sporting a black eye is not the only sign that a bully has been on the prowl; for the one in four workers who are bullied, verbal abuse is the more common complaint and for those on the receiving end working life can become a complete misery. Annie Hayes reports on the costs and issues.

Turning a blind eye costs

'I can take a joke, but things in my office have got out of hand. One person gets the worst of it – emails making fun of him are sent round at least once a week and he won't ask for sugar in his tea any more as it is almost always salt. The final straw came last week. He came back from a few days' sick leave to find the contents of his desk packed in a box. On top was a "sorry you're leaving" card signed by most of the department. Apparently that was "hilarious".'

This was a letter published in *GuardianJobs* earlier this year. For some workers this is the upsetting reality of life at work.

Matt Witheridge, operations manager for the Andrea Adams Trust (the world's first charity dedicated to tackling workplace bullying), says that this type of bullying is typical.

'Physical bullying is very rare – it does occur in some industries where there is manual labour for example, such as construction. More common though is the verbal type – snide comments happen behind the scenes and becomes a form of Chinese water torture.'

According to the Trades Union Congress more than 2 million people are bullied at work every day. Some 18.9 million working days are lost to industry every year through bullying, and it costs individual companies between eight and 10 per cent of their annual profits on top of the threat of costly litigation which is enough to put any employer on red alert.

Last year saw the groundbreaking case of city worker Helen Green who was awarded a whopping £800,000 from former employer Deutsche Bank Group Services on grounds of bullying.

It's not just huge payouts such as these that are hitting businesses hard but also the loss in productivity and absence. And according to research by the Chartered Institute of Personnel and Development (CIPD) employees who are bullied are more likely to be depressed and anxious, to be less satisfied at work, to under-perform and want to quit.

Commenting Mike Emmott, CIPD Employee Relations Adviser, says: 'Bullying and harassment is a serious problem in many workplaces and employers need to take the issue more seriously. It can damage individuals' confidence, morale, motivation and sometimes their health, causing them to be less productive and effective at work. It can also trigger absenteeism, make retention rates go down and both the employer's reputation and bottom line can take a hit.'

It is also a growing problem. Research released last November to coincide with National Ban Bullying at Work Day showed that 15 per cent of union safety representatives said bullying was a major problem in their workplace. That compares with 12 per cent two years ago and 10 per cent in 2002.

Exposing the pest

For Green the bullying came in a very public form. She said colleagues stonewalled her, blew raspberries and told her: 'You stink'. For others it can take a quieter but no less damaging form – in email taunts, whispered name calling and threatening looks. For many businesses, deciding what is and isn't bullying is part of the problem.

The Royal Mail Group, an organisation that knows a thing or two about bullying, illustrate this point well. Their website says the following:

'Have a look at the workplace behaviours below and decide which of them might amount to bullying and harassment.

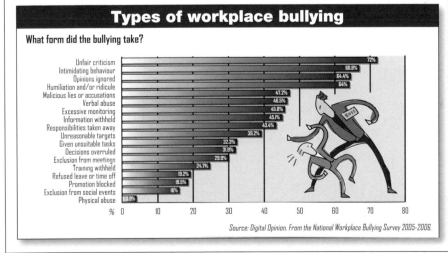

Types of workplace bullying

What form did the bullying take?

	%
Unfair criticism	72%
Intimidating behaviour	66.8%
Opinions ignored	64.4%
Humiliation and/or ridicule	64%
Malicious lies or accusations	47.2%
Verbal abuse	46.5%
Excessive monitoring	45.8%
Information withheld	45.1%
Responsibilities taken away	43.4%
Unreasonable targets	39.2%
Given unsuitable tasks	32.3%
Decisions overruled	31.9%
Exclusion from meetings	29.9%
Training withheld	24.7%
Refused leave or time off	19.2%
Promotion blocked	18.5%
Exclusion from social events	16%
Physical abuse	9.9%

Source: Digital Opinion. From the National Workplace Bullying Survey 2005-2006.

⇨ Shouting?

⇨ Swearing?

⇨ Giving someone too much or too little work?

⇨ Being over critical?

⇨ Jokes or banter?

⇨ Not giving feedback?

⇨ Ignoring someone?

⇨ Suggestive remarks or innuendoes?

⇨ Staring, leering, whistling or suggestive gesturing?

⇨ Display of offensive objects or posters, such as pin-ups?

⇨ Touching or brushing against someone?

⇨ Asking someone out for a date?

⇨ Talking about someone?

⇨ Changing work priorities?

⇨ Not offering proper managerial support?

⇨ Public or private ridicule?

⇨ Comments about dress or physical appearance?

⇨ Standing very close to someone?

⇨ Asking personal questions?

⇨ Sending joke emails?'

The problem, say Royal Mail, is that all of the above are examples of behaviour that may amount to bullying and harassment but at the same time, some of these behaviours might, in the right circumstances, be perfectly acceptable. The conclusion they have reached is that bullying and harassment can be defined as:

'Inappropriate and unwanted behaviour that could reasonably be perceived by the recipient or any other person as affecting their dignity.'

Despite growing awareness of the problem and what it is, the issue still exists. According to CIPD research, 83 per cent of organisations – 90 per cent in the public sector – have anti-bullying policies but still this doesn't seem to be quashing the problem. So who is getting it right and what can businesses learn from them?

Zero tolerance

Witheridge says that policy and procedure only work where they are tailored to the organisation's culture but changing custom and practice is incredibly difficult.

'The key is getting commitment. It has to be led by the chief executive. Lip-service is not enough.'

David Vaughan, Royal Mail's head of diversity and inclusion, explains how they tackled the issue, which resulted in the number of bullying and harassment cases dropping by nearly 20 per cent within the last year:

'The initiatives we have introduced include: setting up a free confidential helpline staffed round the clock by professional, independent counsellors who can give advice and support to any of its people who are concerned about bullying and harassment; improving our complaint procedure if people want to take further action; training everyone in the organisation in diversity awareness; and establishing "Dignity and Respect at Work" groups that provide a forum for people to raise issues.

Some 18.9 million working days are lost to industry every year through bullying

---

'To support the awareness training Royal Mail issued a guide establishing diversity champions across the business to promote inclusion,' he adds.

The NHS, says Witheridge, has also turned things around. 'There is a military hierarchy within the NHS from surgeons down to the cleaners which lends itself to the abuse of large amounts of power. They have addressed this and last year they were one of the main sponsors of Ban Bullying at Work Day.'

According to Witheridge, they have rolled out training in different sites, provided access to advisers and painstakingly written a grievance procedure with meaning.

They've also benefited from some quick-wins. 'Posters are displayed on the backs of toilet doors, which is often the place bullied employees go to cry.'

Sally Humpage, CIPD diversity and employee relations adviser, remarks that bullying is not something that will go away but with awareness growing there are now better ways of dealing with it: 'Employers need to encourage victims to report it, they must make sure policies are followed and provide a positive working environment. The dispute resolution legislation that was brought in a few years ago has at least created some debate on the issue even if it hasn't solved it, and dealing with complaints quickly is often the key. When things escalate, it's often the result of a lack of management training or fear. Employers have to monitor the situation by looking at grievance rates and staff surveys to see where they are.'

Organisations can turn their culture around. The Royal Mail is a gleaming example of how behaviours can be addressed and improved. Bullying and harassment is not a problem that will disappear. As Humpage says: 'The nature of the world we live and work in lends itself to the problem – it's competitive, tough, has long hours and there can be great rewards but with that there is stress and pressure and that often breeds unfortunate types of behaviour. The key is dealing with it appropriately and making sure it doesn't fester.'

19 June 2007

⇨ The above information is re-printed with kind permission from HR Zone. Visit www.hrzone.co.uk for more information.

© HR Zone

Am I a bully?

Information from Connect

We all face pressures at work: sometimes this may lead us to behave in a way which is unacceptable to others without us even realising it. There may also be other non-work-related factors affecting our attitude towards others in the workplace. Often individuals accused of bullying are surprised. It may help sometimes to take a step back and check that our working style is not impinging on others. Below is a brief guide to this process.

Am I a bully?

⇨ Do I use language which is insensitive?

⇨ Do I unintentionally vent my personal opinions on non-work-related matters?

⇨ Do I express anger or dissatisfaction at work, particularly in physical behaviour?

When you may not be feeling yourself is when you are most likely to consciously or otherwise use work channels to vent frustrations from your home life. This is more likely to occur if:

⇨ You are suffering from stress.

⇨ Losing a feeling of control and security over your life, work-related or private.

⇨ Are problems away from work causing you to behave differently whilst there?

What you can do

Positive ways that as a manager you can ensure your behaviour does not run the risk of you being labelled a bully, and that you can promote best practice. Try to:

⇨ Be firm but fair. On occasion it may be you wish to criticise colleagues. Try to avoid harsh criticism, make your point without intimidating or frightening colleagues.

⇨ Avoid frequent outbursts and tantrums. We all face pressure situations at work, it's best to attempt to deal with this with a good old-fashioned deep breath and count to ten than externalising it on to colleagues. This sort of behaviour will automatically land you with the bully label.

⇨ Communicate with your team, assessing together the priorities and workload, perhaps in a relaxed situation over a cup of tea will help reduce the potential for stress and conflict.

⇨ Try not to let favourites develop within your team – try to treat everyone equally so as team members do not feel excluded, encourage everyone to contribute new ideas and give feedback.

⇨ If you have been or feel you are badly managed try to prevent repeating these mistakes.

⇨ The above information is reprinted with kind permission from Connect, the union for professionals in communications. Visit www.connectuk.org for more information.

© *Connect*

Bullying: virtual fighters

BlackBerries and mobiles have blurred the boundaries between work and personal lives, and one unpleasant side effect has been the inexorable rise of 'cyberbullying'. Margaret Kubicek investigates

Microsoft is developing Big Brother-style software that can remotely monitor a worker's productivity. And while gadgets such as BlackBerries and mobile phones were developed with the aim of helping us become more efficient, it seems they can also be used as a means of abuse – providing an 'in' to our personal time and space from which there may seem to be no escape.

The rise of technology in the workplace has another unfortunate side effect: the potential for threatening behaviour between individuals.

This 'cyberbullying' is something employers increasingly need to concern themselves with, and should bring their policies and procedures up to date. This should result in fewer complaints and, where incidents do occur, the ability to resolve them early before they significantly dent employee productivity.

Social networking

Email figures heavily in the vast majority of cases, but those involving social networking sites such as Facebook and MySpace – with their audience of millions – cause perhaps the greatest humiliation and distress.

'With technology and the Internet, it's much easier and less constraining for the bully,' says Cary Cooper, professor of organisational psychology and health at Lancaster University

KEY FACTS

⇨ Since December 1999 all schools must have an anti-bullying policy in place by law. (page 1)

⇨ Research with 11- to 19-year-olds found that one in five young people (20%) had experienced bullying or threats via email, Internet chatroom or text message. (page 2)

⇨ Almost two-thirds (65 per cent) of young lesbian, gay and bisexual pupils have experienced direct bullying. (page 2)

⇨ For six years, bullying has been the biggest single reason for children calling ChildLine, with about 20,000 calls a year. (page 3)

⇨ 35% of a sample of 7- to 18-year-olds say that they have been bullied outside of school. The survey, carried out by BMRB for the ABA with 1,078 7- to 18-year-olds in England, found that the most likely places for children and young people to experience bullying outside school were on the street (16%), on the way to and from school, and in the park (12%). (page 7)

⇨ Young people over the age of 15 reported more bullying than younger children, with one in five experiencing bullying on the streets of their community. (page 7)

⇨ Bullying on the grounds of body image/size/obesity is one of the most prevalent forms of prejudice-related bullying. Recently, the level of such bullying has been exacerbated by national concerns about rising levels of obesity. (page 8)

⇨ 71% of callers telephoning Childline about bullying in 2004/05 were female. (page 10)

⇨ Half of all teachers do not challenge homophobic language when they hear it. (page 12)

⇨ Homophobic bullying and abuse is not exclusively targeted at lesbian, gay and bisexual people, but also at those who are perceived to be lesbian, gay or bisexual, or who do not conform to existing sex/gender codes. (page 13)

⇨ 82% of children and young people with a learning disability have experienced bullying. They are twice as likely to be bullied as other children. (page 14)

⇨ 56% of young people have experienced bullying, but new figures show that over 70% of young people have bullied, quashing the notion of a small minority of bullies wielding power over a majority of victims. (page 18)

⇨ Around 16 pupils in the UK kill themselves every year due to distress over bullying. (page 19)

⇨ Young male bullies are aware of the damage that they cause their victims but carry on to guarantee their own personal gain, according to findings of preliminary research at the University of Sussex. (page 20)

⇨ Less than one per cent of primary school children are 'true bullies', and most children who bully are themselves bullied by other pupils, the researchers say. Bullies are also more likely than their classmates to suffer from low self-esteem, depression, and behavioural problems from early childhood and through primary school. (page 21)

⇨ 46 per cent of teachers said young people who cannot afford the fashion items or branded goods owned by their peers have been excluded, isolated or bullied as a result. (page 22)

⇨ A new study published by online identity experts Garlik charts the number of young net bullies in the UK. One in five 8- to 15-year-olds (18 per cent) freely admit to being online bullies and posting deliberately offensive comments about others and in extreme cases 'stealing' their identities. (page 28)

⇨ With the increase of electronic intimidation, 64% of secondary school teachers say pupils have been victims of cyberbullying, according to a survey carried out by the Association of Teachers and Lecturers (ATL). In addition 16% of teachers have themselves been victims of cyberbullying and of those more than half have received silent calls or been the victims of videoing, which has been posted on websites such as YouTube. (page 29)

⇨ Three and a half million people (14 per cent or one in seven of the workforce) say they have been bullied in their current job according to a YouGov poll for the TUC. 21 per cent (one in five) say that bullying is an issue where they work. (page 33)

⇨ Bullying in the UK is endemic and for one in four people it is a weekly or even daily cause of stress. Over 80% of workers have been bullied during their careers and a third of people are so stressed they have dreamed of quitting for a life abroad. (page 34)

⇨ Some 18.9 million working days are lost to industry every year through bullying, and it costs individual companies between eight and ten per cent of their annual profits on top of the threat of costly litigation. (page 35)

⇨ Failure to tackle bullying in the workplace costs UK employers almost £14bn each year, research has found. (page 39)

GLOSSARY

Bullying

Bullying involves persistently and deliberately harming another person, usually somebody who is perceived to be different or vulnerable. Bullying can be verbal, physical or emotional and can take many forms, including name-calling, teasing, physical violence, having your possessions stolen, having rumours spread about you or being ignored and left out. In all schools, at least 5-10 per cent of pupils will experience long-term bullying – but in some schools this figure will be much higher.

Cyberbullying

Cyberbullying is the use of Information and Communications Technology (ICT), particularly mobile phones and the Internet, to deliberately upset or intimidate another person. The use of this technology means bullies can now reach their victims at any time and in previously safe areas such at their homes. Between a fifth and a quarter of students have been cyberbullied at least once.

Happy slapping

An assault which is filmed and circulated on the Internet or by mobile phone. Happy slapping is a criminal offence. It typically involves a stranger being physically assaulted by an individual while other members of a group use mobile phones to record the attack.

Homophobia

Homophobia is a fear or dislike of gay, lesbian and bisexual (LGB) people and of homosexuality. Almost two-thirds of young lesbian, gay and bisexual pupils at secondary school have experienced homophobic bullying, according to the charity Stonewall. However, homophobic bullying is not restricted only to pupils who are known to be LGB; any pupil who is not perceived as conforming to typical roles and characteristics associated with their gender and sexuality may be victimised.

Learning disability

Somebody with a learning disability may not have developed the academic and social skills usually associated with their age group; they can therefore be a target for bullies, being perceived as both vulnerable and 'different'. According to Mencap, eight out of ten children with a learning disability are bullied.

Prejudice

Dislike of a particular group, race or religion. Prejudice-related bullying often involves abusive behaviour, intolerance or exclusion because of the victim's race, gender, body image/size, sexuality, disability, age or religion.

Sexual bullying

Sexual bullying can include comments about appearance, abusive name-calling, spreading rumours about someone's sexual behaviour, sexual innuendoes and criminal offences such as assault and rape. Sexual or sexist bullying is more commonly directed towards females by males and is often based on a dislike or feeling of superiority towards them and a double standard relating to sexual behaviour. Although more commonly aimed at women and girls, boys can also suffer from sexual bullying, often with a homophobic element.

Workplace bullying

Bullying at work occurs when someone tries to intimidate or humiliate colleague, often in front of other staff. Three and a half million people (14 per cent or one in seven of the workforce) say they have been bullied in their current job, according to a YouGov poll for the TUC.

INDEX

ACKNOWLEDGEMENTS

The publisher is grateful for permission to reproduce the following material.

While every care has been taken to trace and acknowledge copyright, the publisher tenders its apology for any accidental infringement or where copyright has proved untraceable. The publisher would be pleased to come to a suitable arrangement in any such case with the rightful owner.

Chapter One: Bullying Trends

Bullying, © NSPCC, *Expert guide: bullying,* © Community Care, *Children on bullying,* © Crown copyright is reproduced with the permission of Her Majesty's Stationery Office, *Bullying myths and facts,* © respectme, *Survey finds one in three bullied outside school,* © National Children's Bureau, *Prejudice-related bullying,* © NASUWT, *'I was called names like slut and whore',* © Guardian Newspapers Limited, *An inclusive culture,* © ATL, *Bullying wrecks lives,* © Mencap, *Truths we must face up to,* © New Statesman, *70% of kids are bullies,* © Beatbullying, *Are you a bully?,* © BullyingUK, *Study looks at why the bullies carry on bullying,* © University of Sussex, *What is a bully?,* © Institute of Education, University of London, *Bullies, victims more likely to consider suicide,* © Reuters, *The brand-name bullies,* © ATL.

Chapter Two: Cyberbullying

Online bullying, © Becta, *Cyberbullying,* © Crown copyright is reproduced with the permission of Her Majesty's Stationery Office, *A million online bullies run rampant in cyberspace,* © Garlik, *Prevalence of cyberbullying,* © ATL, *Keeping cyberspace safe,* © Crown copyright is reproduced with the permission of Her Majesty's Stationery Office, *Happy slapping,* © BullyingUK.

Chapter Three: Bullying at Work

Bullying in the workplace, © Crown copyright is reproduced with the permission of Her Majesty's Stationery Office, *Three and a half million bullied in job,* © Trades Union Congress, *Workplace bullying rife,* © Samaritans, *The hidden menace: bullying at work,* © HR Zone, *Am I a bully?,* © Connect, *Bullying: virtual fighters,* © Reed Business Information Limited, *Failing to tackle bullying costs employers £14bn,* © Reed Business Information Limited.

Photographs

Flickr: page 31 (Eddie~S).
Stock Xchng: pages 3 (Craig Jewell); 4 (Sophie); 13 (Sanja Gjenero); 14 (Glenda Otero); 17 (Philippe Ramakers); 20 (Ahmed Al-Shukaili); 25 (Craig Jewell); 33 (ilker); 38 (Carl Dwyer).

Illustrations

Pages 1, 11, 23, 30: Simon Kneebone; pages 6, 12, 28, 34: Don Hatcher; pages 7, 19, 29, 36: Angelo Madrid; pages 9, 18: Bev Aisbett.

Research and additional editorial by Claire Owen, on behalf of Independence Educational Publishers.

And with thanks to the team: Mary Chapman, Sandra Dennis, Claire Owen and Jan Sunderland.

Lisa Firth
Cambridge
January, 2009

Additional Resources

Other Issues titles

If you are interested in researching further some of the issues raised in *Bullying Issues*, you may like to read the following titles in the **Issues** series:

⇨ Vol. 158 *The Internet Revolution* (ISBN 978 1 86168 451 6)

⇨ Vol. 154 *The Gender Gap* (ISBN 978 1 86168 441 7)

⇨ Vol. 153 *Sexual Orientation and Society* (ISBN 978 1 86168 440 0)

⇨ Vol. 149 *A Classless Society?* (ISBN 978 1 86168 422 6)

⇨ Vol. 148 *Religious Beliefs* (ISBN 978 1 86168 421 9)

⇨ Vol. 141 *Mental Health* (ISBN 978 1 86168 407 3)

⇨ Vol. 137 *Crime and Anti-Social Behaviour* (ISBN 978 1 86168 389 2)

⇨ Vol. 136 *Self-Harm* (ISBN 978 1 86168 388 5)

⇨ Vol. 135 *Coping with Disability* (ISBN 978 1 86168 387 8)

⇨ Vol. 127 *Eating Disorders* (ISBN 978 1 86168 366 3)

⇨ Vol. 123 *Young People and Health* (ISBN 978 1 86168 362 5)

⇨ Vol. 117 *Self-Esteem and Body Image* (ISBN 978 1 86168 350 2)

⇨ Vol. 115 *Racial Discrimination* (ISBN 978 1 86168 348 9)

⇨ Vol. 107 *Work Issues* (ISBN 978 1 86168 327 4)

For more information about these titles, visit our website at www.independence.co.uk/publicationslist

Useful organisations

You may find the websites of the following organisations useful for further research:

⇨ **ATL:** www.atl.org.uk

⇨ **Beatbullying:** www.beatbullying.org

⇨ **Becta:** www.becta.org.uk

⇨ **BullyingUK:** www.bullying.co.uk

⇨ **Community Care:** www.communitycare.co.uk

⇨ **Connect:** www.connectuk.org

⇨ **Department for Children, Schools and Families:** www.dcsf.gov.uk

⇨ **Directgov:** www.direct.gov.uk

⇨ **Garlik:** www.garlik.com

⇨ **HR Zone:** www.hrzone.co.uk

⇨ **Institute of Education:** www.ioe.ac.uk

⇨ **Mencap:** www.mencap.org.uk

⇨ **NASUWT:** www.nasuwt.org.uk

⇨ **National Children's Bureau:** www.anti-bullyingalliance.org.uk

⇨ **New Statesman:** www.newstatesman.com

⇨ **NSPCC:** www.nspcc.org.uk

⇨ **Ofsted:** www.ofsted.gov.uk

⇨ **respectme:** www.respectme.org.uk

⇨ **Samaritans:** www.samaritans.org

⇨ **Trades Union Congress:** www.tuc.org.uk